WHAT IS THE BIBLE?

IS VOLUME

60

OF THE

Twentieth Century Encyclopedia of Catholicism

UNDER SECTION

VI

THE WORD OF GOD

IT IS ALSO THE

1ST

VOLUME IN ORDER OF PUBLICATION

THE TWENTIETH CENTURY ENCYCLOPEDIA · OF CATHOLICISM ·

Edited by **HENRI DANIEL-ROPS** *of the Académie Française*

WHAT IS THE BIBLE?

By *HENRI DANIEL-ROPS*

Translated from the French by J. R. FOSTER

HAWTHORN BOOKS · PUBLISHERS · *New York*

First Edition, September, 1958   *Fifth Printing*, August, 1959
Second Printing, October, 1958   *Sixth Printing*, November, 1959
Third Printing, October, 1958   *Seventh Printing*, June, 1960
Fourth Printing, January, 1959   *Eighth Printing*, January, 1961

NIHIL OBSTAT

Johannes M. T. Barton, S.T.D., L.S.S.

Censor Deputatus

IMPRIMATUR

E. Morrogh Bernard

Vicarius Generalis

Westmonasterii, die XXV APRILIS MCMLVIII

The Library of Congress has catalogued this publication as follows:

Daniel-Rops, Henri, 1901–
    What is the Bible? Translated from the French by J. R. Foster. [1st ed.] New York, Hawthorn Books [1958]

    128 p. 21 cm. (The Twentieth century encyclopedia of Catholicism, v. 60. Section 6: The Word of God)

    Includes bibliography.

    1. Bible—Introductions.   I. Title.
                                        Real name: Henri Jules Charles Petiot.
    BS475.D273   220.6   58–11591 ‡

CONTENTS

CHAPTER I

THE BIBLE, THE BOOK

OF BOOKS

THE FOUNDATION OF OUR CIVILIZATION

There is a unique and inexhaustible book in which all there is to say about God and man is said. God's presence pervades it and in it are revealed all those aspects of his mysterious being that we are allowed to glimpse; in it he appears, he speaks and he acts. Man can also see himself in it, in all his potentialities, his grandeur and his weakness, from his sublimest aspirations down to those obscure regions of consciousness in which each of us bleeds from the wound of original sin. It embodies above all a religious doctrine, the doctrine of the revealed truth; but human knowledge and intellectual activity also find in it rich and never-failing nourishment. It is as vain to claim to understand the principles of ethics and law as of sociology, economics and even politics if one is unaware of the message contained in this book.

Art and literature are still more obviously dependent on it. But for this book, the sculptors of Chartres, the mosaic-workers of Ravenna, Michelangelo, Rembrandt and El Greco would not be the artists we admire. Still more important and significant than the number of the works which owe their themes to it is the existence, also due to the Bible, of an art that transcends the laws of aesthetics and acquires a spiritual meaning. It is the same with literature. This book praised by Montaigne and Racine, by Shakespeare and Goethe, even by Nietzsche and

Anatole France, has done more than provide innumerable subjects for dramatists; from it flows the stream of living water that feeds the roots of masterpieces. But for the Bible, would there ever have been a Dante, a Racine, a Pascal or a Dostoyevski?

Paul Valéry wisely pointed out that western civilization rests on three foundations: Greek intellectual curiosity, Roman order and Judaeo-Christian spirituality. Let one of these collapse and the whole edifice is threatened with destruction. And of these three foundations the third, and really the most important because it endows the whole structure with its true meaning, is the unique and inexhaustible book which gives it its character and initial impetus. Without it the West would not be what it is.

But to link this book with the existence and development of western civilization alone is to falsify its meaning and limit its range. We can see more and more clearly, as efforts are made to render its message universal, that, by its underlying premises as well as by the modes of expression it employs, it is perfectly suited to mentalities very different from those of Europe, that Asia and Africa can welcome it perfectly naturally and that their genius is even, in a sense, allowed for in it. If the white man must to a large extent thank the Bible for the rôle of guide that history grants him, the coloured races owe to it their awakening to greater light.

Such is *the Bible*, the book of books, the book of man and the book of God.

THE HOLY BOOKS; THE BOOK

The very name we give this book sums up and indicates all its exceptional characteristics. The word goes back beyond its Greek etymology—*biblos* or *biblion*, book—to those distant days in the second millennium before Christ when the Phoenicians of Byblos had made their port the greatest papyrus market of the time and imposed the name of their town on the product that they sold. Its use in the sense we give it, however, only goes back to the fourth century of our era, to the days of St Jerome, who gave currency to the expression "the Holy

Books" or simply "the Books"; in Greek, *ta biblia*. Low Latin turned the word into a feminine and declined it *biblia, bibliae*. And so in everyday usage this plural became a singular, and this collection of seventy-three books was referred to by a word which implies its underlying unity, its supernatural harmony. The synonym that has often been used to describe it, *Scripture* —a term that in fact translates *"the Holy Scriptures"*—expresses in different words the same idea, namely that all the heterogeneous elements of which it is formed coalesce into a higher synthesis.

Scripture, Holy Books, Book, Bible; the different words all correspond to one and the same intention. We are clearly dealing with the unique book, the book *par excellence*, the book that surpasses all other books. It is the absolute in books, because the message it contains is itself the absolute.

THE MOST WIDELY READ BOOK IN THE WORLD

The Bible is also, of all the works of the spirit, by far the most widely read in the world. It is only possible to guess at the number of copies in circulation; the figure of one to two thousand million has been mentioned, and it grows every year by some two million. Even in antiquity the book had begun to spread. The traditional story of Ptolemy Philadelphus asking the High Priest Eleazar to send him the seventy-two best scholars in Israel to endow the library of Alexandria with a Greek translation of the Hebrew scriptures has symbolic value; it proves the fame that the work already enjoyed. The Bible became still more widely diffused when the Christians, having added to the Jewish section the part containing the supreme revelation brought by Jesus, strove to spread it. The Bible was copied in monasteries; the great ones of the earth wanted to have copies. When Gutenberg invented printing, he turned to Scripture for the first text to which he applied the new technique.

Today, the Bible can be read in almost every language of any

importance in the world. Estimates of the number of translations vary from seven hundred and thirty to eleven hundred
and forty. It exists in Japanese and Arabic, in Breton and
Flemish, even in Eskimo and Senegalese. We might perhaps
single out for special mention the year 1817, when it appeared
for the first time in an African language—Malagasy, in point of
fact—whilst Morrison was working on the first Chinese version.
The public for the Book never ceases to expand. In the century
of the "death of God" this success is significant; it confirms the
sovereignty of the Word, of that Word of which it was said that
it would not pass away.

CATHOLICS AND THE BIBLE

Yet it must be admitted that for a long time Catholics lagged
behind in this field. For nearly three hundred years their attitude towards the Book of Books was one of anxious mistrust.
This was one of the consequences of the terrible crisis that
shook the whole Christian world in the sixteenth century and of
the split that is marked in the annals of the Church by the
Protestant revolution. Yet it would not be correct to say that
when Luther, shut up in the Wartburg castle that hid him from
the eyes of his enemies, undertook his great work, the German
translation of the Bible, Catholicism as a whole was showing
no interest in the Scriptures. Between the invention of printing
(1450) and the year (1520) in which the former Augustinian
monk set to work, one hundred and fifty-six Latin editions of
the Bible had appeared and, to mention only Luther's own
country, seventeen versions in German. There can be little
doubt, however, that these publications were intended almost
solely for specialists, that the common people had scarcely any
access to them and that the Book "which ought to have been,
night and day, in the hands of devout men, lay only too often
buried in dust". The simultaneous decline of interest in the
Bible and the liturgy from the end of the thirteenth century
onwards corresponded closely with that break-up of the ideal
of Christendom of which the rise of nationalism in politics, the

development of nominalism in theology and the relaxation of morals were other symptoms. Save for that decline, Luther's attack would have had no significance and its results would not have been what they were.

But when Luther and, with him, the other "reformers" gave back to the Book its supremacy and lustre, they committed the irreparable mistake of separating it from the tradition which had guaranteed its text and contributed so much to its elucidation. Having become man's only source of faith and spiritual life, the Bible provided a means of doing without the Church, its social organization, tradition and hierarchy. The Catholic Church was quick to see the danger of this break in the historical evolution of the Christian message and of this conversion of belief into a matter for the individual conscience. It reacted with the protective measures taken by the Council of Trent. The most important of these forbade the faithful to read Scripture in vernacular translations which had not been approved by the Church and were not accompanied by commentaries in conformity with Catholic tradition. Excessive caution, perhaps, combined with an influence not untinged with Jansenism, endowed this prohibition with an absolute character that it never possessed. It became common to hear it said: "The Bible is on the Index", or "A Catholic must not read the Bible". The Modernist crisis at the beginning of this century, when imprudently directed studies called in question the authenticity of Scripture, helped in no small measure to strengthen this suspicious attitude.

All this involved a serious loss for Catholics. How could one be fully Christian after cutting oneself off from the very roots which have allowed the Christian faith to live and blossom? It has been the especial merit of popes in the last sixty years to measure the extent of the loss and to remedy it. Three great encyclicals restored the rights of the truth—and of the Bible: *Providentissimus Deus* of Leo XIII in 1893; *Spiritus Paraclitus* of Benedict XV on the occasion of St Jerome's fifteenth centenary in 1920; and the illuminating message of Pius XII in 1943, *Divino afflante Spiritu*, which was the starting point of the present biblical revival. At the same time several bodies were either created by the Holy See or founded with its encouragement. Among them were the *Pontifical Biblical Commission* (1902), which lays down the teaching of the Church in matters of Scripture,[1] and the Pontifical Biblical Institute (Jesuit) and the Biblican School of Jerusalem (Dominican), which are responsible for pursuing and directing studies in this field. The Benedictine monastery of St Jerome, in Rome, was given the task of revising the Latin translation of the Scriptures, the most important one as it is in Latin that the sacred texts are used in the Roman rite.

From now on, the Catholic Church says to her children, "Read the Bible!" And in every country in the world in which her authority is recognized considerable efforts are being made to obey this injunction. In France alone, six translations, one sixty years old but recently brought up to date, one twenty years old and four other more recent ones share a public that grows daily greater.[2] One of them, recommended by Cardinal Liénart, has sold more than three hundred thousand copies in four years. Today, therefore, it is perfectly easy for Catholics to obey

[1] A few words about the decrees of the Biblical Commission. Its decrees have lately been republished (*Enchiridion Biblicum*, 1954); at the same time its secretary and deputy-secretary published a note emphasizing (i) the *historical* bearing of the decrees (they must be interpreted according to the circumstances of their publication) and (ii) their specific nature (a distinction must be made: "We have in mind two kinds of decisions. It is possible that a decree is connected with faith and morals; in so far as it is so connected, it naturally retains all its authority and remains binding. But very often the decisions of the B.C., by the very nature of their subject, have no connection with faith and morals. The Commission has generally intervened in questions of a historical or critical nature. In questions of this kind new evidence may re-open a question which might have seemed settled. . . ."). (Article by Dom Jacques Dupont, O.S.B., "A propos du nouvel Enchiridion' Biblicum", in *Revue Biblique*, July 1955, pp. 414–19.)

[2] For details of modern English translations of the Bible, see the bibliography at the end of this book. The most important are Mgr Knox's version (from which, unless otherwise indicated, quotations in the text are taken), the Westminster Version and the new American translation, known as the "Confraternity version", now in course of publication. [*Trans.*]

the instruction of Canon 1391 and to read the Bible only in authorized editions. As for the number of publications devoted to the Bible, it is staggering: nearly two hundred works and a host of articles in French alone in 1954.

These efforts and their results have their significance. The sacred text is no longer a prey to the whims of free examination and private judgement. Handed on to the faithful by Mother Church herself, who interprets it according to the wisdom of a tradition that stretches back twenty centuries, Holy Scripture has once more assumed its rôle of living link and inexhaustible source. Reading the Bible is no longer, as it may have appeared to some of the sixteenth-century heresiarchs to be, a personal adventure, a revolt against authority, tradition, the hierarchy and established dogma; it is a lofty act of faith and loyalty.

Thus Holy Writ appears as a decisive factor in the twentieth century's choice between faith and the refusal to believe. Henceforth there is one section of humanity which lives by Scripture, by the Book of Books, and another which rejects it, because henceforth there is one section of humanity which can conceive of a life without God and another that makes him, as the Bible does itself, the *Alpha* and *Omega*, the beginning and end of all things.

CHAPTER II

FROM THE SPOKEN WORD
TO OUR "BIBLES"

THE BOOK WAS FIRST THE SPOKEN WORD

How were these books, which together form the Bible and which we regard as the foundations of our faith, composed and handed down to us? Our modern "bibles" hide under their uniform appearance not only the amazing diversity of their component parts but also the mystery of their origins. Who thinks, as he thumbs the closely printed pages, of the time when these words and sentences were not fixed in cold print but chanted or intoned to audiences by the voices of the Heralds of God?

Long before it was a written text, by far the greater part of the Bible was oral teaching. In the form of more or less stereotyped narratives, rhythmic and assonant poems, and pithy proverbs and sayings, its elements were handed down from generation to generation by the spoken word before the use of writing became general. This rather special kind of genesis, of which other oriental books (the Koran, for example) provide examples, is intimately related to the cultural, spiritual and linguistic patterns of the people among which the Bible grew up, patterns of a simple and communal type in which literary creation was much less individual and intellectual, and more living and spontaneous, than among us. To understand properly how the Bible arose, we must forget the habits we have acquired as modern men and members of a paper civilization. Reading and writing have become such automatic operations that it is difficult for us to realize that some societies have been able to manage almost entirely without them. Our memory has become bloodless and barren, and our faculties of improvisation have more to do with mere words and rhetoric than poetry and prophecy. In ancient Israel, right up to the time of Christ, it was very different. The ability to speak with fluency, art and a gift for aphorism was the mark of those who today would be "writers". The trained memory was a superb tool. "A good disciple," said the Jewish Scribes, "is like a well-made cistern; he does not let a single drop of his master's teaching escape."

Transmission by memory and the spoken word was greatly facilitated by the technique applied to it. There was an art of learning by heart that formed part of the art of composition. This oral style has left a visible mark on the text; the written version to a large extent preserves its patterns. The regularity of the rhythm, the repetition of certain words and the use of alliteration assisted memory. We have only to read aloud many passages in the Gospels to become aware of the oral phrasing behind the written text. In the verses

> You would not dance when we piped to you,
> You would not mourn when we wept to you,
> (Luke 7. 32)

we are obviously confronted with a rhythmical fragment, a sort of refrain.

Sometimes we know for certain that the teaching existed before it was written down; the prophecies of Jeremias were *spoken* twenty-two years before they were committed to writing. All the prophetical books, all the psalms and all the poetical parts, especially the Song of Songs, which is a collection of wedding hymns, obviously possess this character. Even in the historical books we may suspect from the tone and from various turns of phrase that we are dealing with spoken chronicles, rather like those with which Homeric bards and medieval minstrels alleviated the boredom of the nobility.

This does not mean that written elements did not exist. The

Bible itself alludes to collections, like the *Book of the Wars of Yahweh* and *The Book of the Just*, which must have been familiar to everyone, to judge by the way in which they are mentioned. "Is it not written in the Book of the Just" (Josue 10. 13) how Josue, to win time to make his victory complete, ordered the sun to stop and was obeyed? Today, after the innumerable discoveries of archaeology from Sinai to Ras-Shamra, no one denies the existence of very old biblical writings earlier in date than the tenth, perhaps even than the twelfth, century. At the time when Moses' Hebrews were in Egypt, writing had been in general use on the Nile for fifteen centuries. However, these written elements were for long only aids to memory before they were incorporated in the compilation that we possess.

Curiously enough, the process was the same with the New Testament books, or at any rate with the Gospels; the Acts of the Apostles, the Epistles and the Apocalypse are written documents presented as such. Some, like St Paul's letters, were dictated, and in these the "oral style" reappears. The Gospels were certainly first "spoken" before they were written down. The first generations of Christians attached enormous importance to this oral teaching. Imagine a child of today being told by his grandmother that her own grandmother used to talk to her, when she was a little girl, about Napoleon, and tell her how she had seen troops marching past just before Waterloo; surely that direct memory would seem much more concrete and real than anything he could read in his history book? For at least four or five generations Christians heard the Gospel as a story handed down, by word of mouth, by unimpeachable witnesses. About A.D. 130—that is, at a time when the four evangelists had long published their books—St Papias, Bishop of Hierapolis in Phrygia, declared that what he preferred to anything else, where tradition was concerned, was "the living and enduring word". A little later St Irenaeus, at Lyons, recalled the days when he used to listen to St Polycarp, the great Bishop of Smyrna, telling what he had heard himself from St John the Apostle. The

Gospels preserve the tone of these living witnesses; that is what is so moving about them.

However, the need to guide those who handed on the Gospels and the wish to avoid deviations, errors, exaggerations and distortions eventually made it necessary to have recourse to writing. Behind the final text of the four little books the reader can still sense the "notes" that the evangelists used at first.

THE TRIUMPH OF WRITING

The transition from oral to written transmission poses a number of problems. The first is that of date: at what point did the text assume its written form? For the Old Testament, only a cautious reply can be given to this question. There were, it seems, three periods of intense literary activity. In the time of Ezechias the oral or written records of the Southern Kingdom were probably collected, put into order and compared with those of the Northern Kingdom, which Samaritan scholars who fled to Jerusalem in 722 B.C. brought with them (cf. Prov. 25. 1). In the reign of Josias the famous "discovery" of Deuteronomy took place and the first complete version of the Pentateuch may have been put into writing. The work seems to have been completed soon after the return from exile, when Cyrus, in 538, allowed "the remnants of Israel", the exiles in Babylon, to return to their country and to set up a sort of little state under Persian protection. Just as Nehemias, in about 445, rebuilt the walls of Jerusalem, so another great man erected the spiritual citadel, the Bible: the wise scribe Esdras, lawyer and theologian combined, was reputed to have miraculously dictated ninety-four holy books and to have made his whole people follow their precepts. So it was apparently in the fifth century that the old fragmentary versions were collated, the orally transmitted parts written down and these various elements arranged in a coherent whole. A century earlier, at Athens, Pisistratus had lent his name to a similar operation on the Homeric poems. To this original Bible was subsequently added a small number of texts referring to the centuries that followed and recording fresh spiritual attainments.

The facts concerning the second part of the Bible, the New Testament, are better known. It has already been mentioned that the Acts of the Apostles, the Epistles and the Apocalypse make it clear in so many words that they are written or dictated texts; so far as they are concerned, therefore, no problem arises. As for the four Gospels, the transition from word of mouth to writing took place at various dates, for different reasons and under different conditions. Without going into the details of learned discussions, the composition of the Gospels may be summarized as follows. Papias says: "Matthew was the first to put down the sayings of the Lord, in the Hebrew tongue." So the first of the "evangelists" was apparently the former tax-gatherer of Capharnaum, who probably wrote his Gospel between 50 and 55 in the language spoken by the Jews at that time, that is, Aramaic. Soon afterwards St Peter, who was in Rome, was joined by Mark, a young Jew who knew Greek; as he listened to the Prince of the Apostles, this intelligent young man noted down what he heard, compared his notes with the little aids to memory already in circulation, and between 55 and 62 produced his Gospel. It was in popular Greek and obviously addressed to the Christian lower classes of Rome all round him. Almost at the same time a well-educated doctor, Luke, who had been St Paul's companion on his travels, arrived in Rome. He had learned much from the Apostle of the Gentiles and during his stay at Jerusalem had gathered first-hand information, perhaps from the Virgin Mary herself. In due course he wrote his Gospel, in excellent Greek and in the first place for the rather more distinguished people who gathered round Paul. Either the success of these two new accounts or even that of his own Aramaic one induced Matthew to complete and translate his own work, probably soon afterwards, between 64 and 68. As for the fourth Gospel, St John's, it was written at Ephesus by the beloved apostle at the end of his long life, some considerable time after the first three. It is a mixture of reminiscence, documentation and spiritual meditation and is usually reckoned to date from the last few years of the century, perhaps from about 96–98.

This brief summary has shown in what languages the Bible was written. There were three. Hebrew, the original, sacred language of God's people, is used in the vast majority of the parts that are the fruit of the Jewish tradition; it was to remain the liturgical language of Israel up to our day, and the Dead Sea discoveries have proved that the Essenes were still using it round about the beginning of our era. Aramaic, a related Semitic language, was always gaining ground at the expense of Hebrew in everyday use, so much so that it may have been this that forced Esdras to fix the text of the Scriptures; in Christ's day everyone used it. But there are only a few books in Aramaic in the Bible: Matthew's original Gospel, as we have seen, and certain parts of Esdras, Daniel and Jeremias. Greek was little used before the time of Christ—only the second book of Machabees and that of Wisdom were written in this tongue— but when our era began its use was so widespread that to all intents and purposes all the sacred books of the Christians were written in Greek—popular Greek, by the way, which was by no means always identical with the language of Homer or Plato.

There remain two practical questions: on what material and in what writing was the text of the Bible recorded? Two materials were used. One, which was cheap, consisted in the fibres of the papyrus, the Egyptian reed, crushed and held together by a coating of varnish; this was the origin of paper. The other, which was much dearer, was parchment, that is, the carefully tanned and pumiced skin of an animal. Originally the leaves of papyrus or parchment were fastened end to end in rolls; the Jewish liturgy has remained faithful to this practice. The custom of sewing the leaves together in groups of four pages—each group was called a *quaternion*, from which is derived the French word *cahier*, copybook—which were then assembled in a volume, dates from the second century before Christ and was popularized by the Christians.

As for the scripts employed, they varied enormously during the course of the centuries. Early Hebrew was not written in the massive, square letters that it employs today; this script only took shape in the centuries immediately before Christ. The archaic letters were more like the Phoenician alphabet. Neither form of writing included the signs and dots which in present-day Hebrew indicate the vowels. Greek was more or less as we know it today, except that the old copyists did not separate the letters or use any punctuation, which often makes it difficult to read. Needless to say, in both languages the writing varied in quality. Sometimes it is the careful calligraphy of the "publishing firms", at others cursive and rapid, with the words all joined together. This kind of writing does not make any easier the ticklish problem of the transmission of the texts down the centuries before the invention of printing, that is to say, the notorious problem of the manuscripts.

MANUSCRIPTS OF THE BIBLE

It is hardly necessary to say that we do not possess any original manuscript of the books of the Bible, any more than we do of Homer or Pindar. We know them only in copies. Thousands of manuscripts of the Bible exist; they are far from being catalogued. In 1780 a Hebrew scholar by the name of Kennicott boasted that he had personally collated 261 manuscripts of the Jewish Bible and examined 349 others; whereupon one of his rivals, the Italian de Rossi, retorted with the assertion that in his own library alone he had 310 copies that the Englishman had never seen. As for the value of these extremely numerous manuscripts, their interest obviously varies tremendously according to their date and the care taken in copying them.

In speaking of an ancient text one must never lose sight of the elementary fact that until the invention of printing the written word was handed down by a succession of copies. Each time it was copied the text ran all kind of dangers; the scribes might be careless, ignorant or so eager to do a good job that they "emended" the original in accordance with their own ideas. As for the "revisers" who intervened from time to time to restore the text to its original purity, it often happened that their boldness or lack of comprehension produced further blunders. Consequently, our chances of possessing an accurate copy of an ancient text diminish with the passage of time. It is not generally known that in the case of the great classical writers the interval between composition and the first known manuscript is almost always enormous: fourteen hundred years in the case of the tragedies of Sophocles and the same for Aeschylus, Aristophanes and Thucydides; sixteen hundred years for Euripides and Catullus, thirteen hundred years for Plato and twelve hundred for Demosthenes. How great is this interval in the case of the Bible?

So far as the Hebrew part is concerned the reply until recently was fairly pessimistic. No manuscript earlier than the ninth century was known. The oldest seems to be that of the synagogue at Karasubazar, near Simferopol in the Crimea, which has been dated at A.D. 830. The Leningrad Bible, also discovered in the Crimea, is dated in "the year 1228 of the era of the Seleucids". Antiochus the Great reigned in Syria from 223 to 187 B.C., so this manuscript would date from about 1000. The divergencies between different copies of the Hebrew Bible are in any case very slight, because in very early medieval times the Rabbis gave careful attention to the task of fixing the text and its pronunciation by the addition of vowel points. The result of their labours is known as the *Massora*.[1] As many as possible of the manuscripts earlier than this Massoretic revision were destroyed and only small fragments of them are still extant.

The situation has been modified by the recent discoveries in the neighbourhood of the Dead Sea. It is well known that in 1947 rolls containing many biblical texts were found hidden in jars in a cave. The subsequent exploration of neighbouring caves brought still more rolls to light. It is generally agreed

[1] *Massora* means tradition in Hebrew. The work of the Massoretes extended from the sixth to the tenth century. Up till then vowels had not been indicated in the Hebrew text of the Bible. [*Trans.*]

that they formed the library of a nearby Hebrew monastery belonging to the strict sect of the Essenes and were hidden in these caves during the terrible events of the Jewish War of A.D. 66–70. It goes without saying that the texts must be earlier than this date, and some of them seem to be a great deal earlier, dating perhaps from the third or even fourth century B.C. For the parts of the Bible which occur in the "Dead Sea Scrolls", therefore—notably two complete copies of Isaias and parts of Genesis, Deuteronomy and Exodus—we now have copies extremely close to the original. The question arises whether comparison with previously known manuscripts will lead to important modifications in the received text. First reports suggest that it will not. The text of Isaias is apparently almost identical with ours.[1]

When we come to the books of the New Testament the problem is much more complicated. We are confronted with innumerable copies of every age differing greatly in character. They may be divided into three classes: minuscules, uncials and papyri. The minuscules are all later than the ninth century; by this time the text had been standardized and, apart from a few details, they reproduce the "received text". The most famous manuscripts are those copied between the fourth and ninth centuries in that noble script known as uncial. At least two date from the fourth century: the *Codex Vaticanus* (at the Vatican) and the *Codex Sinaiticus*, which was found at the monastery of Sinai among old parchments that had been cast aside, taken to Russia and sold by Soviet Russia to the British Museum. The *Codex Bezae* at Cambridge dates from the fifth century. It fell into Protestant hands at Lyons and was given to the University of Cambridge in 1581 by Theodore of Beza, Calvin's famous disciple. So the interval between the originals and the copies of the Christian books is one of only three or four centuries; of the great classical writers, only Terence and Virgil are in this happy position.

[1] See *Les Manuscrits hébreux du Désert de Juda*, by A. Vincent (Paris, 1954) (or *The Dead Sea Scrolls and their Significance*, by H. H. Rowley (London, 1955) [*Trans.*]).

What is more, the sands of Egypt have yielded papyri (which were often used for wrapping mummies) covered in writing. Among these invaluable documents are several fragments of the Gospels and Epistles. The most noteworthy papyri are the Egerton papyrus, the Chester Beatty papyri and those acquired by the University of Michigan. The biggest fragment gives us St Paul's letters almost in their entirety. The most precious of all is the Rylands papyrus, which is to be seen at Manchester. It contains a passage from chapter 18 of St John's Gospel and dates from about A.D. 130, that is, it is almost contemporary with the original. The case is unique in the whole history of ancient texts and proves how swiftly the Gospel spread.

By comparing all these manuscripts with one another it is possible to arrive at a text that may well be completely authentic. It should be added that we have another indirect check at our disposal, that provided by translations.

ANCIENT TRANSLATIONS OF THE BIBLE

Today we read the Bible in translation. Only professional biblical scholars go back to the original text, to the great Hebrew edition by Rudolf Kittel of the Stuttgart Biblical Institute (Stuttgart, 1937) or to the Greek editions of the New Testament by Nestle (Stuttgart, 1898–1941) or A. Merk and the Pontifical Biblical Institute (Rome, 1948). The Bible was translated into other languages at a very early epoch, and the interest of these old translations is considerable, for they enable us to reconstruct the texts used by the translators, which are often earlier than those preserved by our manuscripts.

The first in date of these translations, and one of the most famous, is the Septuagint. We have already seen that it was made in Egypt—in the third and second centuries before our era—according to the legend at the request of an enlightened pharaoh, in fact because the Jews of Alexandria, ill-acquainted with Hebrew, needed a translation. This Greek version was an outstanding success. The first Christian communities used it and almost all the translations into other languages were made from it. Some of the Fathers of the Church, St Augustine for example, thought that it was "inspired". Modern scholarship, however, has subjected this illustrious work to close examination and, while emphasizing its great interest, pointed out that some of the translators made mistakes or paraphrased the text. However that may be, the fame of this translation ousted all the other Greek versions, for example those of Aquila (c. A.D. 140) and Theodotion (c. A.D. 180), of which Origen thought highly.

The Gospels had scarcely been published before translations of them were made, particularly into the two languages most used (together with Greek) by the primitive Christian communities, Syriac and Latin. The Latin versions are obviously of prime importance, first because they occur in a large number of very old manuscripts, and second because it was through the medium of Latin that holy Scriptures became part and parcel of western civilization. One is famous above all others, the Vulgate of St Jerome. But before the great scholar set to work numerous Latin versions had been made, especially of the Gospels, often differing considerably from each other and no doubt based on very early texts. Only about fifteen manuscripts of these earlier versions are extant. The two most famous are in Italy. One is at Vercelli (it belonged to Eusebius, who was bishop of this city and died in 371) and the other at Trent, the Palatinus, which also belongs to the fourth century. The triumph of the Vulgate caused the older translations to be discarded.

St Jerome lived from 347 to 420, first at Rome and afterwards in a solitary hermitage at Bethlehem. On the advice of his friend Pope Damasus, he resolved to endow the Church with as perfect a translation as possible of the holy books. For the New Testament, he limited himself to a careful and detailed revision of the existing text; for the Hebrew Bible, he undertook the monumental task of making a translation direct from the originals. St Jerome's Vulgate, living, warm and often picturesque, has had a profound effect right up to the present day on the reading of the Bible by Christians. It even eliminated from everyday use versions which had their value, like the revision made by St Augustine. Copied from generation to generation, until the invention of printing, the Vulgate suffered the common fate of texts copied by hand. After the Council of Trent an official edition was compiled, on the orders of Clement VIII (1592–1605). The Benedictine monks of the Abbey of St Jerome in Rome are now at work on a more scientific revision.

Recent translations of the Bible into modern languages almost all take into account the Septuagint and the original Hebrew or Greek as well as the Vulgate.[1] In the last fifty years an immense amount of energy has been devoted to the task of sifting the text. We certainly possess a more "authentic" Bible than the Christians of days gone by.

TEXTUAL CRITICISM

This task is governed by textual criticism, a meticulous science with exacting laws of its own. Amid the multiplicity of variants, that is, more or less divergent readings, it is no easy matter to arrive at the truth. Some idea of the complexity of the problem may be gained from the knowledge that, in the four Gospels alone, there are upwards of a hundred thousand variant readings. Most of them, of course, only affect details, sometimes a word or even only a syllable or letter, but that does not make collation any easier.

Textual criticism employs methods which, when all used simultaneously, form a touchstone of authenticity. External criticism studies and compares the manuscripts. It has to decide whether the better of two variants is the one given by a hundred manuscripts that may all have copied the same original, which itself perhaps contained a mistake, or the one given by one single manuscript that seems better guaranteed. So for each text

[1] Of modern versions in English, Mgr Knox's is a translation from the Vulgate. The Westminster Version and the Confraternity Version of the Old Testament are translations from the original tongues. For further details of these versions, see the bibliography. [*Trans.*]

an attempt must be made to reconstruct the history of its transmission. This is not always possible. In that case we must turn to internal criticism, which tracks down obvious errors by making use of the context. It tries to detect whether such-and-such a reading interrupts the train of ideas, has been influenced by another text (this is quite frequent in the Gospels), or conflicts with the author's genius and modes of thought and writing. It can easily be imagined that the whole science is an extremely delicate one and that its results are often only conjectural. Thanks to its patient efforts we can rely on having as faithful a text as possible. But it should be emphasized that, on the whole, these variants only affect very small points, tiny details even, and that it is rare for discussion of them to call in question important truths. Taken as a whole, the text of holy Scripture as we possess it today is quite sufficiently sound and well guaranteed to form a basis of faith.

CHAPTER III

THE "CANON" OF THE
TWO TESTAMENTS

A COMPLEX AND APPARENTLY HETEROGENEOUS BOOK

It must be admitted that the reader's first impression on open-ing the Bible and turning over its pages will be one of amaze-ment. Chateaubriand confessed as much in a famous passage of his *Genius of Christianity*. What is the meaning of this heterogeneous collection of books differing from each other in kind, in tone and in intention? It is as if the *Song of Roland*, a code of canon law, Joinville's *Chronicles*, *Cyrano de Bergerac*, some interesting bits from Michelet's *History of France*, two or three of Voltaire's *Philosophical Tales* and some anthologies of poetry had all been strung together.[1] Any attempt to detect a less formal kind of unity, to discover a style common to all the books or even to all the authors would be futile. Some parts of the book flash with the sparkle of genius, others are undeniably platitudinous and dull. Yet the astonishment aroused by a merely superficial glance at the Bible is nothing, as we shall see, compared to that produced by a consideration of its contents or any attempt to take them all literally.

The reader must overcome his initial discomfiture and seek

---

[1] An equivalent list from English literature would juxtapose items like *Beowulf, the Anglo-Saxon Chronicle, Henry the Fifth*, selections from Macaulay's *History of England*, two or three essays from the *Spectator* and the *Golden Treasury*. [*Trans.*]

the aid of introductions and commentaries (there are many good ones today) which will prevent his losing his way in this maze. Above all, he must try to grasp the grand idea binding all these diverse books together. To regard the Bible as a collection of heterogeneous texts ranging from cooking recipes to the highest mystical speculations is to condemn oneself to complete incomprehension. On the other hand, everything appears in a fresh light and falls into place when you realize that, taken as a whole, the Bible is a history, the history of a unique people whose destiny followed a divine plan. From the literary point of view it is absurd to talk of the "plan" of the Bible; yet everything in it, even the mostly unlikely looking passages, has its part to play in God's plan.

HOW TO FIND A BIBLICAL REFERENCE

When a text from the Bible is quoted, it is normally followed by a reference consisting of letters and figures, in most cases an abbreviated word, a roman numeral and an arabic numeral (but sometimes two arabic numerals, which is not so clear). We might come across, for example, Jer. vii, 15 (Jer. 7. 15) or Mt. ix, 7 (Matt. 9. 7), which mean, "Book of the Prophet Jeremias, chapter seven, verse fifteen" and "Gospel according to St Matthew, chapter nine, verse seven". These simple indications immediately point to an interesting fact: the division of the Bible into books, chapters and verses. This division is certainly useful, for its triple nature enables us to pin-point immediately any given passage, but it is questionable whether the breaks it involves, whose artificiality is obvious as soon as we start to read continuously, do not form a tiresome interruption to the train of ideas and even occasionally make the narrative hard to understand.

The division into books designated by a title (Book of Kings, Exodus, Epistle to the Romans, or Apocalypse), by the name of their author (Jeremias, Isaias, Matthew, Mark) or by that of the principal character in them (Tobias, Job, Ruth) is bound up with the conditions under which the Bible grew up, that is, with the problem of choice, which we are going to tackle in a moment. The other divisions are of lesser importance and in any case of much more recent origin.

The chapters, which are of approximately equal length, only go back to the beginning of the thirteenth century. The credit for this innovation belongs to Stephen Langton, a professor at the University of Paris and later Archbishop of Canterbury and a Cardinal. It was a great success; Parisian scribes made it fashionable and from 1226 onwards it spread everywhere. The Jews themselves adopted it with only small differences. The present chapter divisions are still those made by the learned English cardinal.

As for the division into verses, it is comparatively recent, just four hundred years old. The celebrated Parisian printer Robert Estienne introduced the famous little figures that mark—and sometimes chop up—the sentences when he brought out an edition of the Bible in 1551. The method governing the division defies rational analysis; sometimes a clause is cut in two, at others two quite unconnected statements are put together. Very often it looks as though purely typographical reasons were at the bottom of it. However, the procedure has been so long sanctified by usage that in practice it is impossible to abolish it.

THE TWO "TESTAMENTS"

The first and most important division in the Bible is the one which divides its books into two portions of unequal length known as the Old Testament and the New Testament. At first sight the word "testament" looks ambiguous; in French and in English it has a very precise meaning which it seems difficult to apply to the books of the Bible. Yet, rightly understood, it confronts the reader immediately with the mystery at the very heart of Scripture, that of the covenant between God and man through the intermediary of a people, that is, it confronts him with the divine plan.

For testament simply denotes *alliance*, the Hebrew word

berith applying to the Covenant which existed, from the time of the call heard by Abraham, between the Almighty and the People which he had appointed to be his witness and mouthpiece. *Berith* was rendered in Greek in the Septuagint by the word *diatheke*, which lays emphasis on the idea of treaty or document sanctifying the alliance (the term *suntheke* would have been more appropriate and was in fact used by other less illustrious translators). In Latin, *diatheke* was translated by *testamentum*, a term which denoted "a written document of an official character", that is, treaty of alliance as well as will.

In the former sense it describes first of all the special relations of God with his people, but it can also refer to the union which God himself, putting on a human form, sealed with man by the sacrifice of Christ. So there is an Old Covenant and a New Covenant, as the Gospel often repeats. And surely the latter includes the second meaning of the term. For, as the Epistle to the Hebrews says (9. 15–22), it is by the testator's death that the heirs enter into possession of his goods, and it is by Christ's death that the children of God gain access to their eternal heritage. In the most tragic sense of the term, testament expresses man's right to the divine adoption secured for him by the sacrifice of Calvary; the New Covenant is sealed with blood.

THE "CANON", THE RULE OF FAITH

In each of the two main parts of the Bible there are a certain number of texts or Books. Why are they there? Because the Church declares that they express authentically and properly the Alliance of God with man in its two forms. This is the idea denoted by the usual term Canon and not, as is often thought, simply that of "list" or "catalogue".

The word is Greek, but probably borrowed from some Semitic tongue; in Hebrew *qaneh* means a measuring reed, the one of which Ezechiel speaks (40. 3, 5). It was employed by the Alexandrian grammarians for the corpus of classical works worthy of serving as models, by Cicero in the same sense, by

Pliny, with reference to the sculptor Polyclitus,[1] to denote the right methods to follow in making statues, and by Epictetus to describe the moral rules of the good life. The Fathers of the Church in large numbers, from St Clement of Rome to St Hippolytus, used the word to denote anything fundamental to religion: the rule of tradition, the rule of faith or the rule of truth. Quite naturally the sense was extended to cover any writing that laid down a rule; a text was called "canonical" when it fixed rules of belief or action; hence, by extension again, the sense of "collection of writings laying down the rule". When in 350 St Athanasius said of the *Shepherd of Hermas*, "It is not part of the Canon", it was in this sense that he understood the term. From that time onwards it became current; St Jerome, St Augustine and St Gregory Nazianzen all use it.

It is in this sense that down the centuries many of the official documents of the Church have taken it, among the most important being the decisions of the Council of Trent in 1546 and those of the Vatican Council in 1870. So the "canon" of Scripture comprises all the books proclaimed by the Church as "regulating faith"—and at the same time "inspired", a qualification which depends, as we shall see, on another criterion. The list is henceforth unalterable; let us see how it was settled.

THE CANON OF THE OLD TESTAMENT

The list of "canonical" books is the one drawn up by the Council of Trent at its fourth session. It comprises forty-five books: Genesis, Exodus, Leviticus, Numbers, Deuteronomy (these first five together form what is known as the Pentateuch), Josue, Judges, Ruth, two books of Samuel, two books of Kings, two of Chronicles, Esdras, Nehemias,[2] Tobias, Judith, Esther,

[1] One of his most famous statues, the *Doryphorus*, a youth carrying a spear, was in fact known as "The Canon" or standard. [*Trans.*]

[2] Some of these books have alternative names: 1 and 2 Samuel and 1 and 2 Kings are also called 1, 2, 3 and 4 Kings; Chronicles are called Paralipomenon and Nehemias is also known as 2 Esdras. These are the names used, for example, in the Rheims-Douay and Knox versions. [*Trans.*]

Job, Psalms, Proverbs, Ecclesiastes, Song of Songs, Wisdom, Ecclesiasticus, Isaias, Jeremias (with Lamentations), Baruch, Ezechiel, Daniel, Osee, Joel, Amos, Abdias, Jonas, Micheas, Nahum, Habacuc, Sophonias, Aggeus, Zacharias, Malachias (these last twelve are known as the Minor Prophets) and two books of Machabees. The Jews (followed by the Protestants) only recognize thirty-eight of them; even in the time of Jesus they were not agreed on the canonicity of all the holy books, some—the most numerous and strictest—accepting only those in Hebrew, the others wishing to include seven other books generally preserved in Greek, Tobias, Judith, Wisdom, Ecclesiasticus, Baruch and the two books of Machabees, not counting some parts of the book of Esther only extant in Greek. For a long time now, or at any rate since the thirteenth century, Catholics have divided the Old Testament into four main parts: the Pentateuch (which the Jews call the Law, the Torah), the Historical Books (Josue to Esther together with Machabees), the Poetical and Sapiential Books (Job to Ecclesiasticus) and the Prophetical Books (Isaias to Malachias).

The next question that arises is how the canon of the Old Testament was formed, that is, how the religious leaders of Israel, the chief priests and doctors of the Law, decided what was "canonical". There is absolutely no doubt (the fact is attested by the Jewish historian Flavius Josephus, who lived from 37 to about A.D. 100) that in the time of Christ, apart from the differences mentioned above between strict Jews and more liberal, hellenizing Jews, there existed a properly drawn-up list of the scriptures, a "canon"; it contained the thirty-eight books, a figure which was sometimes artificially reduced to twenty-two, the number of letters in the Hebrew alphabet. But as for the criteria and methods that the rabbis used in making their choice and the dates when they made it, these are questions to which we can give no precise answers. It seems to have been King Josias (639–609 B.C.), in whose reign the high priest Helcias "found the Book of the Law in the house of Yahweh", who first established a still very short and rudimentary canon. Anyway, from the fifth century onwards there was a list of sacred books read in the synagogues; Esdras drew it up about 444 B.C. The prophetical group seems to have been fixed somewhat later, perhaps about the third century B.C. The Book of Psalms, which enjoyed great prestige because of its attribution to the royal poet David and its use since time immemorial in the liturgy, must have long formed part of the canon by natural right, as it were. The other, so-called "hagiographical", books were put together by scribes and scholars during the third and second centuries, and the list must have been finally settled after the famous persecution of Antiochus Epiphanes (175–164 B.C.), when Judas Machabeus ordered a search for the sacred rolls that had escaped destruction in order to collect them together. So by and large it does not look as though there was ever an official verdict, comparable to the decision of a General Council, declaring the Old Testament as a whole canonical.

The canon did not pass into Christian use without numerous discussions and hesitations. The general principle was to regard as canonical the books quoted by Jesus and the Apostles, but in practice this did not work. It would be true to say that the Fathers of the Eastern Church tended to favour the smaller Hebrew list, while the Western Fathers admitted the deuterocanonical books that the Jews had finally excluded. In the fourth century the situation was still fluid; St Hilary refused to grant the seven books in question the title of "canonical", but considered them nevertheless as part of Holy Scripture. It seems to have been St Jerome and St Augustine who, by rallying to the cause of the wider canon, secured its triumph in the Church. The councils of Hippo (A.D. 393) and Carthage (A.D. 397), and a letter of Innocent I in 405, prove that by that time the canon was fixed as we know it today.

THE CANON OF THE NEW TESTAMENT

So far as the New Testament is concerned, Protestants are more or less in agreement with Catholics, except that they are not so categorical in their attributions; for example, the Epistle to the Hebrews, to which Catholics affix St Paul's name, remains in their eyes of problematical authorship. But the number of books is the same for both: twenty-seven. They are divided into three sections: the historical books (the four Gospels and the Acts of the Apostles), the didactic books (the fourteen epistles of St Paul and seven other epistles with the signatures of St Peter, St John, St James and St Jude) and finally one prophetical book, the Apocalypse.

It should not be thought that this new canon was rapidly fixed by an *ex cathedra* decision. It was much more a matter of common assent, amid the inspired fervour of those primitive churches which were close to the revelation and still nourished the flame of the Holy Spirit. The decision arose from practice, quite naturally and calmly. There were certainly hesitations, second thoughts and perhaps discussions. Eusebius tells us that Serapion, bishop of Alexandria, confronted with a Gospel according to St Peter, at first authorized it to be read, then, having examined it closely and found traces of the Docetist heresy in it, forbade its use. The Shepherd of Hermas, that attractive early second-century book, was for some time considered to be inspired; then it was removed from the canon by the West, but remained in favour in the Egyptian Church.

What is certain is that the Church used extremely rigorous methods in making its choice. Tertullian tells us, about A.D. 200, that some thirty years earlier, in the province of Asia, a book known as the Acts of Paul had appeared, telling how the Apostle converted a young pagan girl called Thekla, who then began to preach the Gospel admirably. Tertullian goes on to say that the story looked suspicious, its authorship was investigated, and the writer, a priest more well-intentioned than wise, immediately deprived of his position. In any case, we have only to read the so-called "apocryphal" books and to compare them with the canonical writings in order to see where good sense, moderation and wisdom are to be found and how tactfully Scripture fixes and limits the bounds of the supernatural and the marvellous.

The two criteria which decided the choice were essentially catholicity and apostolic nature. A text was admitted to the Canon when, in the Christian communities as a whole, it was recognized as faithful to the true tradition and the true message. As the liturgy crystallized, the custom of reading pages from the Epistles and Gospels during Mass exposed their contents to a public test; when the Christian conscience, illumined and guided by ecclesiastical authority, had recognized a certain number of them as bearing the mark of the Holy Spirit, the choice was made. And as in these primitive communities the apostolic connection was fundamental, those writings were retained which living testimony established as emanating directly from the disciples of Jesus.

In any case, towards the close of the second century the choice had been made. We possess an extremely precious document that proves it, the Muratorian Canon, so called after Muratori, librarian of the Ambrosian Library at Milan, who discovered and published it in 1740 in the version preserved in a manuscript of the sixth or seventh century. This document simply reproduces a catalogue or list of the Scriptures compiled at Rome about A.D. 200. It shows that at that time the Roman Church had the same canon as the Christian Church of today (except for the Epistles of St James and St Peter), and that it rejected the Shepherd of Hermas (which it authorized to be read, however) and more categorically certain writings of gnostic tendencies. Some hundred and fifty or two hundred years later, between 359 and 400, catalogues of the canon grew more numerous; they have been found in Africa, Phrygia, Egypt and at Rome. The Council of Carthage in 397 drew up a definitive list. "The first article of our faith", said Tertullian, "is that we are to believe nothing beyond what is contained therein." The decree of the Council of Trent at its fourth session in 1546 only confirmed this list, to which Eastern Orthodox Christians decided to subscribe in 1672.

A STRANGE WORLD: THE APOCRYPHA

So the canon is the result of a choice willed and guided by the Holy Spirit, and it becomes clear that the Bible is the residue of a considerably larger literary production which we are far from knowing in its entirety. The recent discoveries in the neighbourhood of the Dead Sea have revealed to us the existence of a non-biblical religious literature of strikingly high quality; some of the fragments already published—the Commentary on Habacuc, the Psalms of Thanksgiving, the Manual of Discipline, the War of the Sons of Light and the Sons of Darkness—would not be unworthy to take their place by the side of many books in the Old Testament.

The books excluded from the Canon are known as *apocrypha*; the word originally means "hidden, secret, esoteric", but as the heretics of the gnostic sects had a passion for the esoteric, a tendency to which the genius of Christianity was hostile, anything based on any kind of so-called secret became suspect, and "apocryphal" came to mean "condemned by the Church".[1]

There are Old Testament apocrypha, compiled between 300 B.C. and A.D. 100, that is, at a time when the Jewish community was painfully enduring the tyranny of various pagan conquerors. Originating in an atmosphere of anguish, they reflect a state of intense spiritual fermentation; some persist in giving a distracted commentary on the Law; others are appeals to a purer, loftier moral life, a rebirth of souls; the last, and the most numerous, offer the escapism of *Apocalypses* (*apokaluptein* in Greek means to uncover), by revealing the approach of the end of the world, when the elect of God will receive justice; the *Psalms of Solomon*, the *Ascension of Isaias* and the *Sibylline Books* are among the best known of these.

As for the New Testament Apocrypha, they form a curious

---

[1] Protestants do not employ the same terminology as Catholics. They use the word *apocrypha* to denote the seven books retained by the Catholic Bible and called by Catholics *deutero-canonical*, that is, later than the Jewish canon. They call the Apocrypha *pseudepigrapha*, because they almost all borrow the names of famous people as pseudonyms.

world in which snippets of truth float on a sea of delirium. These books, which arose in the primitive Christian communities from the earliest days up to the sixth or seventh century, are the products of pious curiosity about anything to do with our Lord, the fondness of the masses for a good story and sometimes of suspicious heretical intentions. We have so-called gospels according to St. James, St Matthew, St Peter and even according to Nicodemus, infancy gospels full of details about the first years of Jesus, accounts of the Assumption of Mary, and pseudo-acts of the Apostles and apocalypses attributed to Peter or Paul. The Middle Ages were very fond of these stories; art made use of them and many were collected in Jacques de Voragine's *Golden Legend*. They would scarcely have any more than historical interest if it were not that many present-day customs had their origin in them; for example, that of putting a donkey and an ox on each side of the crib in which the infant Jesus sleeps.

CHAPTER IV

THE BOOK IN WHICH
GOD SPEAKS

INSPIRED BY GOD

The Catholic Church (and conservative Protestants, too) attributes to all the books composing the Bible the special character of being inspired. That is an essential premise, a premise of faith: the whole Bible is an inspired book. "As sons of the Church", writes Lagrange, "we must believe this with divine faith. If the Church imposes this belief on us, it is because she has the power to do so, and it is only by her authority that we can have certain knowledge on this point." The idea is in any case contained in the various expressions used to describe the Bible: Holy Books, Holy Scripture, "divine literature" (Tertullian), "divine library" (St Jerome), Holy Bible. And the first words of the most recent encyclical on the biblical question, that of Pius XII in 1943, say just the same thing: "Divino afflante Spiritu", "Inspired by the Divine Spirit, the sacred writers composed the Books which God wished to give to the human race . . .".

So the Bible is the Word of God addressed to men, the Word in writing. The Church received this certainty from Israel, where it had existed from time immemorial. Since the Hebrew people knew that it had been chosen by God, that there was a Covenant between the Almighty and itself, and that its whole history formed part of a divine plan, it was natural that the book in which, together with this history, the instructions and appearances of God were recorded should be regarded as inspired. Had not God revealed himself to Abraham in his unique divinity? Had he not commanded Moses to write down his words and thus fix the law? Had it not been the same with the Prophets? Yahweh's words to Jeremias were true of all of them: "Into thy mouth I put my words" (Jer. 1. 9). So the Jewish historian Flavius Josephus is summing up what was nothing less than a dogma when he emphasizes that all the authors of the Book wrote "inspired by God".

Christians have always said, and continue to say, the same thing. Formulas affirming the same faith are continually on the lips of Jesus and the Apostles. It was really God who spoke to Moses (Mark 12. 26; John 9. 29; Acts 7. 44; Rom. 9. 15); it was he who expressed himself through the Prophets (Luke 1. 70; Acts 3. 18); he even spoke through the mouth of the royal poet David (Acts 1. 16; 4. 25). The elliptical phrase in the Epistle to the Corinthians is categorical and significant: "God has told us so" (2 Cor. 6. 16). "Everything in the scripture has been divinely inspired", proclaims St Paul again to his friend Timothy (2 Tim. 3. 16), and St Peter teaches: "It was never man's impulse, after all, that gave us prophecy; men gave it utterance, but they were men whom God had sanctified, carried away, as they spoke, by the Holy Spirit" (2 Peter 1. 21). It is pointless to quote the Fathers and Doctors of the Church; texts repeating and affirming the idea are too numerous. The *Enchiridion Biblicum*, published at Rome in 1935, collects quotations from the popes and councils stretching over nearly two thousand years. What Leo IX wrote in 1053 corresponds exactly to what Pius XII wrote in 1943; what the Council of Lyons proclaimed in 1274 is identical, word for word, with the decrees of the Council of Trent in 1546 and of the Vatican Council in 1870. The teaching of the Catholic Church has never wavered.

WHAT INSPIRATION MEANS

It is clear, however, that the term inspiration needs to be defined. Nothing could be more mistaken than to imagine the

Bible as a miraculous work originating somewhere or other in some mysterious fashion and suddenly appearing even more mysteriously among men. Opponents of Christianity have sometimes reduced the doctrine of inspiration to this bare outline in order to ridicule it. "The Bible", says Mgr Weber, the Bishop of Strasbourg, humorously but wisely, "is a divine book, but it did not fall from Heaven ready made."

The precise definition of inspiration is to be found in St Thomas Aquinas: "The Holy Spirit is the principal author of the Scriptures, men were his instruments" (Quodl. 7, art. 14), a statement which has been expanded in Leo XIII's encyclical *Providentissimus Deus*: "Inspiration is a supernatural impulse by means of which the Holy Spirit excited and moved the sacred writers to write and helped them whilst they wrote in such a way that they could conceive exactly, wished to report faithfully and expressed with infallible accuracy, all that God commanded them to write and nothing else." A wise and penetrating definition which, in the production of the sacred books, leaves room for God's power on the one hand and man's intelligence and will on the other.

The Lord did not write the Bible himself in the same way that his visible hand outlined on the wall of Balthazar's palace the famous warning words: *Mane, Thecel, Phares.* He did not dictate it to a succession of mediums in trances, as the Greeks thought was the case with the Pythia[1] of Delphi. Even the paintings which depict an angel whispering in an evangelist's ear the text which he is in the process of writing, although admissible in a symbolic sense, run the risk of giving a false idea of the phenomenon. To bring the Bible into existence the Holy Spirit used as his instruments men; and each of them retained his personality, his distinctive characteristics, his talent or genius, his habits of thought and his stylistic ability. He did not destroy or infringe on the faculties of those whose function it was to put his message into words.

It should be emphasized that one of the most important

[1] The priestess of Apollo, who replied, usually in incoherent or ambiguous words, to the questions put to this famous oracle. [*Trans.*]

results of pontifical teaching in the last sixty years, from *Providentissimus Deus* to *Divino afflante*, is to have made possible a clearer conception of the rôle played by man as God's instrument in the phenomenon of inspiration. Many so-called difficulties, absurdities or contradictions which "free" criticism claims to meet in the study of the Bible disappear when one takes account of this rightful division between the divine work and the human task. Today, Renan would have considerable difficulty in enumerating those famous conflicting truths of the Bible which alienated him from the faith.

IF THE LORD SPEAKS, WHO SHALL RESIST?

Let us consider the three phases of the phenomenon, as defined so well by Leo XIII. God *excited and moved* the sacred writers to write; they did not buckle down to the task of their own free will, as profane writers do (although literary "inspiration", so often referred to, is to some extent the secular reflection of authentic inspiration).

This aspect of the phenomenon is particularly striking in the case of the Prophets and everything connected with prophetic inspiration. There are innumerable passages in Scripture showing the irresistible effect of the Spirit on anyone possessed by him. The Spirit "pounces" on him, says the book of Samuel, and "enters into" him. The person inspired can only say what Yahweh dictates to him. God "opens his eyes" or ears. The prophet cannot escape the task he is inspired to perform. As Amos, Jeremias and many others said from personal experience, "If the Lord speaks, who shall resist?" We all know how Jonas paid for refusing to carry the word of the Lord to Nineveh. There we have a struggle between the will of God and the will of man which must ultimately be regarded as a mystery of faith.

Scriptural inspiration is similarly, if less clearly, dependent on the divine will. It does happen that sacred writers refer to their sources, exactly as a modern historian would (1 Kings 11. 41; 14. 19, 29; Prov. 30. 1), or even admit that their literary labours have been painful (in the Prologue of Ecclesiasticus, for example, or in 2 Mac. 2. 24, 32); the Jewish tradition and with it the Church's belief declare that the action of the Holy Spirit was just as decisive in this case as in that of the commands thunderously dictated to the Prophets, different though the method employed may have been.

GOD CANNOT ERR

In the second place, according to the Encyclical, God enlightened the intelligence of those whom he chose as his mouthpieces; and he did it in such a way that, while giving full play to their human faculties, he conferred on the work divine value. This supernatural enlightenment must be understood in two ways. On the one hand, God revealed "secrets" to those who had to transcribe his message; this is recorded of Samuel, Daniel, Amos and many others; St Paul in a famous passage even said that he had learnt things "which man is not allowed to utter". This divine illumination does more than open fields of knowledge to the human mind; the inspired writer's judgement, while remaining his own judgement in so far as he is a man, has also become divine judgement through God's supernatural action indissolubly united to man's action.

This is a doctrinal point of capital importance, for with it is bound up the dogma of *biblical inerrancy*, which Fr Benoît, of the Biblical School at Jerusalem, defines in these words: "God cannot be deceived or deceive us. His word is always truth. So if he moves a man to write in his name, he cannot allow him to teach what is false. The charisma[1] of inspiration is necessarily accompanied by the privilege of inerrancy. That is an article of faith which the Church has always professed."

As for the limits of this "inerrancy", it is not enough to say that, taken as a whole, Scripture teaches us the truth. Inerrancy must be understood as an integral property of the whole Bible,

---

[1] I.e. spiritual gift. Charisma is a Greek word meaning *grace* or *favour*; in the New Testament it has the particular meaning of *a free gift of God's grace*. See especially 1 Cor. 12. [*Trans.*]

since the Bible is the work of God and God is truth itself. This inerrancy exists both *de facto* and *de jure*, and every part of Scripture enjoys it. The Biblical Commission, in a decision of June 18th, 1915, came to this conclusion: "What the sacred author asserts, enunciates or conveys indirectly must be regarded as asserted, enunciated, or conveyed indirectly by the Holy Spirit." So a Catholic is absolutely forbidden to hold the belief that inspiration, and consequently inerrancy, is limited to certain parts of the Scriptures, for example to the dogmatic and moral parts, and that, so far as the rest is concerned, we are at liberty to exercise our critical judgement. He is also forbidden to hold the belief that there can be errors of fact in the perspective adopted by the sacred writer; for example, that in one of the biblical books presented as history there can be historical errors. Such is the doctrine of the Church in all its clarity and force.

THE SCRIBES OF GOD

Yet "side by side with this doctrine, an obvious fact, which we can all observe, forces itself on our attention: the Bible, as well as being a divine book, is at the same time an authentically human book" (Mgr Weber). That is, it is a work written by men of flesh and blood like ourselves, living at a definite point in time, against a well-defined historical background, with all the reactions, modes of thought and even prejudices of their civilization. The question arises whether inspiration affects everything about them, even the smallest details of their style. If the essential premises, the basic concepts proceed directly from the Holy Spirit, can it be said that he also determined the choice of words, expressions and sentences? In discussing purely human literature it is, of course, extremely difficult to separate the pure thought from its expression. God must be present at the formulation, the committing to writing of his message; that is what is called "verbal inspiration", which was admitted in general by theologians and exegetes, but not universally, and in any case has never been defined as dogma in an official document of the Church.

Papal teaching takes very much into account the human conditions under which the message was written down. Obviously
"an error must not be imputed to the sacred author where
copyists, in carrying out their work, have made some slip"
(*Divino afflante*); but it is also essential to take into account
the conditions under which the sacred writers lived and their
personal habits of thought and expression. The Lord spoke
through a man, so it is permissible and even necessary to make
ourselves familiar with this man. This is the direction that the
great majority of biblical studies have taken at the moment; it
is well known that it was part of the genius of Fr Lagrange, the
celebrated founder of the Jerusalem Biblical School, to have
foreseen that therein lay the solution of innumerable difficulties.
Serious study of the Bible can henceforth no longer be separated from that of the period and place in which the book was
written.

So inspiration is seen to be a divine operation, a sort of grace
which permeates the sacred writer's whole being, illumines and
guides him, helps him throughout his mental work, from the
impulse to write, the original idea, to the literary execution and
sometimes even the formal expression, but leaves scope for the
reaction of the writer's personality on the work. "The book of
God and the book of man", says Mgr Weber of the Bible, and
the phrase aptly summarizes the whole question.

CHAPTER V

THE BOOK DELIVERED
TO MEN

THE LAND OF THE BIBLE

To understand the sacred text, then, it seems to be essential to know the conditions in which men, inspired by God, wrote the Bible. Let us look first at the geographical conditions, those of the country in which the episodes of the Old and New Testaments took place. "Geography and chronology are history's two crutches", asserts an old university saying, and that applies to sacred history, too, and the whole study of the Scriptures.

The land of the Bible is above all Palestine, that tiny piece of territory no bigger than Brittany, easily crossed in a car from north to south in one day, where the modern traveller is amazed to find the distances so short. It is that strip of land along the shore of the Mediterranean which is so narrow and yet divided by its geology and contours into three very different parallel zones, the maritime plain, the mountains (not very high, but craggy and rugged) and the trench—the *ghor*—in which the Jordan descends to the Dead Sea, some 1200 feet below sea level. It is that region with a half-Mediterranean, half-desert climate, where spring is short but delicious and the summers blazing hot, where the rain falls, between October and May, for whole days at a time in a heavy downpour and yet only too often in insufficient quantity. It is the land where the red anemones grow, the "lilies of the field" of Scripture, where the

Aleppo pine, the cypress, the holm-oak, the carob-tree and the olive cover the plains or mark out the hills, and the rearing of sheep and goats holds a preponderant place in rural economy. But the land of the Bible is also much more than Palestine; it is the "fertile crescent", that band of rich plains encircling the Syrian desert from Galilee via the land of Aram, at the foot of the Anti-Taurus,[1] to the Mesopotamian basin, the huge arc followed by Abraham on his inspired migration.

Geography and the habits of life imposed by it are so intimately bound up with the sacred writings that it is very often impossible to understand the latter without reference to the former. When the Gospel shows us Jesus taking pity on the crowd which has come to hear him and has nothing to eat, we must visualize that region of steppe-like hills overlooking the Lake of Tiberias from the west, where there was certainly no food to be found. When Scripture says, "The rain fell and the floods came and the winds blew . . ." (Matt. 7. 25), to explain the causes of the catastrophes that carry away houses, we must think of the terrible storms which, in that region where all the river-beds are of pebble, do in fact cause raging torrents to overflow their banks. In the bay of the Lake of Tiberias, between Ain Tabgat and Magdala, where the cold waters of the Herman and the warm waters from the springs of Capharnaum meet, a great abundance of fish is to be observed; it seems likely that this is the site of the miraculous draught. When Christ gives the clue, "A man will meet you, carrying a jar of water" (Mark 14. 13), it means nothing to us Westerners, but a detail like that puts the seal of truth on the story, for in Palestine it was, and still is, the housewife's job to fetch the water from the fountain. When he reproaches the Pharisees for giving the tithe of *aneth* and scorning higher obligations, it should be realized that this plant, bitter fennel, was so common in Palestine that no one thought anything of it; today we should say, "give a tithe of weeds". Perhaps Renan goes too far when he declares that Palestine is "the fifth Gospel"; but we must cer-

[1] I.e. the south-eastern end of the Taurus mountains in eastern Asia Minor. [*Trans.*]

tainly pay attention to the evidence given by the Promised
Land on the events it witnessed.

THE AUTHORS

If the geographical background has left its mark on the text
of the Bible, the same is true to an even greater extent of the
personalities of its authors. The problem is not quite the same
as it would be today; the Ancients had no sense at all of literary
ownership, and any piece of writing, being in their eyes the
property of the community, could be revised, modified or continued. It is therefore not always possible to discover one man
behind a biblical text, and certain parts of the Bible give the
impression of expressing the collective conscience and of being
also a collective work, in which each of the writers suppressed
his own personality in favour of the task to be accomplished.

There are, however, numerous cases where the Bible visibly
bears the deep impression of the men who wrote it. The impression is sometimes pleasant, sometimes less so: inspiration
does not prevent the author of Leviticus from being the most
boring of lawyers, the compiler of Chronicles from being totally
devoid of talent or the author of the Apocalypse from making
many syntactical mistakes in his Greek. On the other hand, we
frequently meet powerful personalities expressing themselves in
a very personal style, in fact real literary geniuses. The "King
David" who wrote the Psalms is a sublime poet; the author of
Job is at the same time one of the profoundest and boldest
thinkers the human race has produced and a stylist with a
striking turn of phrase; the prophet Isaias is a real genius, to
be placed on a level with the loftiest lyric poets; and St Paul
spontaneously throws out combinations of words and ideas like
flashes of lightning. Each of these masters of biblical literature
allows us to form an impression—even when he is anonymous
—of his personal character. In the New Testament it leaps to
the eye: Mark is a simple, unspoiled spirit, near to the people,
Luke a cultivated, sensitive man of an inquiring disposition,

John essentially a mystic and Matthew an honest and reliable narrator.

The social surroundings to which these authors belong influence them. Ezechiel and Jeremias, born into priestly families, do not possess the same reactions as Jesus Ben-Sira, a middle-class citizen of Jerusalem, to whom we owe Ecclesiasticus. The author of Job was probably a great sheikh of the desert regions or at any rate on familiar terms with one of these lords of the tent. A provincial like Micheas does not hide how much he hates the big city, which he sees as the very seat of Judah's iniquity. A useful comparison may be made between the imprecations of Isaias (3. 16–24) and those of Amos (4. 1, 3) in the denunciation of female coquetry and luxury; the violence is the same in both cases, but the prophet Isaias is well-born, and remains polite even in his invective, while that ill-educated cowherd Amos allows himself to refer to the fashionable women of Samaria as "cows"—"cows of Bashan", in point of fact—and to inform them that they will be carried off naked and cast into the dung-pit. It is obvious, too, that the place and the date of writing can be very important; the book of Judith reflects the fanatical epoch of the Machabees, and that of Esther corresponds to the mentality of the Jews dispersed throughout Persia, the empire which was to produce the tales of the *Arabian Nights*, of which the story of Esther often reminds us.

Finally, it is surely clear that the style of the biblical writers was liable to vary according to the audience they were addressing. This is particularly striking in the New Testament. Jesus talking to the peasants of Galilee and the fishermen of the lake used a vocabulary familiar to them; he referred to plants, animals and customs they knew. When Luke wants to hand on the message to Roman circles, he has to complete the Master's words here and there, to explain certain details; for example, he has to make it clear that the Jordan is a river and that the Lake of Tiberias is as big as a sea. When St Paul speaks to the Corinthians, who were mad on the Isthmian games, he borrows his comparisons from the sports of the time, wrestling and running; but to the Christians of Phrygia he speaks of their religious speculations. St Athanasius noticed this long ago: "We must note the occasion on which the Apostle spoke, to whom and for what reason he wrote; we must give these circumstances scrupulous and devoted attention, lest by being unaware of them or failing to understand them properly we miss the real sense."

TRADUTTORE, TRADITORE?

It goes without saying that one of the most important factors to take into account in any consideration of the conditions in which the text was written is the language used by the author. Nothing could be more futile, or in a sense more absurd, than arguments turning on the actual words of Scripture in English or some other modern language, when the basis of the discussion is a translation, and often a translation of other translations. The famous verse in the Gospel about the camel and the eye of the needle provides a good example of these interminable but useless discussions. Each of the three languages used by the chosen people, literary Hebrew, conversational Aramaic and popular Greek, known as the *koine* (which was employed in the first Christian communities) had its own genius, its own turns of phrase and expressions, which very often cannot be translated into our modern western languages. The old proverb *Traduttore, traditore* holds good in this case, too; even when he goes straight back to the original, the translator of the Bible always runs the risk of being false to the text.

Apart from anything else, numerous purely idiomatic Jewish terms, translated word for word, can only remain obscure to a westerner of the twentieth century, while they were perfectly clear to a Semite of the time of Christ. How many people today know that throughout the Bible the heart is regarded not as the seat of the emotions but of the intellect; the feelings were reckoned to reside in the loins. So "God searches loins and hearts" means "God sees into the feelings and thoughts of men". Similarly the horn was the symbol of strength; so when, in St Luke (1. 69), the priest Zacharias prophesies that "God has raised up for his people a horn of salvation", he means to announce that a powerful Saviour is going to appear.

More generally, it is the genius of the language which often makes it difficult to understand the sacred text. The most common stylistic tricks of the Semitic languages, parallelism, juxtaposition of propositions and antithesis, are fundamentally different from ours. All three correspond to the dialectic peculiar to the Semitic genius, which is a stranger to the syllogism dear to Greek thought and does not seek to abstract, but aims at seizing the idea in its reality and its unity, even if the result is apparently complex and contradictory. The symbol, which holds an important position in it, does not perform the purely superficial function which it does in our western languages, in which it is scarcely more than a stylistic ornament, or at the most a means of making oneself understood; for the Semites, the symbol is a real sign, which effectively contains within itself a higher reality. When we read that Israel "brings forth the Messias", the word must be understood in its strongest sense; it signifies the whole Promise made to the chosen people and its whole vocation.

LITERARY FORMS OR GENRES

The Bible must be understood according to the language— that is to say, actual tongue and style—in which it was written, but also according to the point of view adopted by the sacred writer; the effort to grasp this point of view is perhaps even more important, and its successful accomplishment in recent years has resulted in the solution or disappearance of a large number of so-called difficulties in the Bible. The most useful contribution to scriptural studies was probably the official recognition by the Church of the existence of literary *genres* and of the necessity for taking account of them.

Anybody with the smallest experience of the written word knows perfectly well that a poet, a novelist, a philosopher and a historian do not use the same registers. The reader instinctively adapts himself to the kind of book he is reading; we do not sit down to read a novel in the same frame of mind as a historical work, and obviously we do not demand from a verse epic the strict accuracy of a military report. It may happen that the same writer uses entirely different registers according to his subject-matter; obviously Shakespeare does not write *The Comedy of Errors* in the same tone as *King Lear*. Each kind of literature has its own laws and customs.

It is the same in the Bible, in which the most diverse *genres* appear side by side; the primitive, popular history of Genesis, the political history of Kings and Machabees, the apologetic history of Chronicles, the moralizing history of Ruth, Tobias and Esther, the collected maxims of Proverbs and Ecclesiasticus, the philosophical essay in dramatic form of Job, the poetry of the Song of Songs and the still more elevated poetry of the Psalms; all these *genres* co-exist in the Old Testament. In the New Testament, we have only to think of the difference between the three Synoptic Gospels and that of St John or between one of St Paul's Epistles and the Apocalypse. If the biblical writers, charged with the task of passing on what had been revealed to them, did so in accordance with the particular genius of the *genre* which they each employed, then the first duty of anyone reading the Bible is to know what kind of literature confronts him. Poetry and song are just as valuable evidence as the historical narrative or the philosophical essay, but they are not the same thing and must not be confused with them, as St Thomas Aquinas warned us. Obviously when we read that, in their Messianic joy, "the hills leap up like sheep", no one takes this poetic formula as the expression of a historical reality.

The question becomes more complex when we come to deal with kinds of literature which the West simply does not possess. For example, a first reading of the Prophets or of the Apocalypse—and even the tenth or hundredth reading in the case of the latter—certainly leaves us feeling somewhat baffled. In Israel, a rather special *genre* was very popular, the *midrash*, a sort of moral fable which was expected not so much to report accurately concrete facts as to exemplify some inner, transcendent truth; to apply to this kind of writing the rules of historical criticism is to risk going seriously astray. The chapters with which the Bible begins, the book of Genesis, obviously belong to a complex species of literature in which history, popular tradition and folklore, moral teaching and cosmogonical revelation are all mixed together and borne aloft on the wings of admirable poetry. As for the actual history to be found in the Bible, it is perfectly obvious that it does not obey the often ridiculously artificial criteria of the "historical science" of today.

The conclusion that emerges from a study of the different kinds of literature in the Bible is that the whole Bible is true, absolutely true, every part of it, but that it is true in the sense in which each kind of literature bears witness to the truth.[1] On this very point the encyclical of Pius XII, *Divino afflante Spiritu* —and more recently, with regard to Genesis, *Humani Generis* in 1950—sheds fresh and piercing light. "It is absolutely essential", says the papal document, "for the exegete to go back to some extent in thought to those distant centuries in the East, so that, making use of the resources of history, archaeology, ethnology and the other sciences, he can discern and recognize what varieties of literature the authors of those ancient times meant to employ and in fact really did employ."

[1] This reference to literary *genres* authorizes liberties which, fifty years ago, would have amazed exegetes and theologians. Dom Célestin Charlier, a Benedictine monk of Maredsous, in *La Lecture chrétienne de la Bible* (Maredsous, 1951), a work published under the Imprimatur of the Bishop of Namur with a preface by Mgr Weber, Bishop of Strasbourg, does not hesitate to write: "The books of Ruth, Tobias and Esther and also, though in a different way, the book of Jonas, belong to the category of works of edification and include obviously fictitious elements" (he prudently adds, it is true, "but for all that we are not entitled to treat them purely as novels in the modern style"). Elsewhere, again, he writes: "The stopping of the sun by Josue is told in a miniature epic poem and looks very much as though it is only an eastern hyperbole."

CHAPTER VI

THE BIBLE AND HISTORY

THE RECORD OF A PEOPLE

That a document of this sort should affirm the usefulness of historical science for the knowledge of the Bible is something quite new and extremely important. Only a hundred years ago the historical problem did not even arise with regard to Holy Scripture, believers limiting themselves to seeking in it religious and moral instruction and unbelievers treating it as myth; today a tremendous effort is being made to discover and establish clearly the historical foundations of the Bible. That is one of the two aims pursued by biblical studies at the moment: to situate the sacred text against its background and to relate the events reported in it to those of profane history. And at once, supported and buttressed by chronology—history's other crutch, the reader will remember—the great episodes of the Bible cease to be the more or less mysterious stories they were reckoned to be not so long ago and become chapters in a history as precise and well-defined as that of the Pharaohs or the Roman Republic.

So the Bible is in the first place a history. It is the record of a people, in fact the most remarkable record a people has ever left, for future generations, of all it did, suffered, believed, thought and hoped. It is the record of a family, Abraham's, kept for about two thousand years, the record of a family that from the Patriarch to Jesus can be followed in its human destiny as well as in its providential mission. That is what gives unity to the Bible and all its heterogeneous parts.

Now it happens that this family, which became a clan and

finally a people, was caught up in the vast series of historical events of which the eastern Mediterranean, Asia Minor and Mesopotamia were the scene. Several times Israel was on the march, from the banks of the Nile to those of the Euphrates; and Palestine, a corridor where the roads from north to south and from east to west cross, was often invaded. All the peoples we know from the ancient history of the East, Chaldaeans, Hittites, Phoenicians, Egyptians, Assyrians, Greeks, Scythians and Romans, were successively in contact with the People of the Promise. The question that comes to mind can therefore receive a reply based on documents outside the Bible itself. And the question is, what is the historical value of this record? Can its evidence be taken seriously?

THE ARCHAEOLOGISTS' REPLY

The reply is given by the archaeologists, those advance guards of the army of historians. Hollot used to say to his pupils at the French School in Athens, "Ancient history is written with a pick-axe". Since, a hundred and fifty years ago, Emile Botta, French consul at Mosul, thought of digging into the oblong "tells" of sand and clay scattered all over the Mesopotamian plain and brought to light the dead towns sleeping under them, the archaeological horizon has never stopped widening. In our day, Fr Poidebard has put the aeroplane at the service of historical science, and aerial photographs taken in the evening when the setting sun casts long shadows reveal undulations invisible from the ground. Even Geiger counters lend their precision to measure the passage of time. The secrets of the buried past are revealed in greater numbers every day.

The modern historian of the Bible draws material from two fields of inquiry. On the one hand, he investigates as an archaeologist the actual sites of events described in the Scriptures, for example the remains of Jericho or traces of the Hebrews' journey through Sinai. Among the most illustrious achievements are those of the Biblical School at Jerusalem, founded in 1890 by Fr Lagrange, whose pupils are carrying on his work. Some of the discoveries in Palestine itself are of the first importance; the uncovering, for instance, in the foundations of the convent of Our Lady of Sion, of the "Lithostroton", the actual paving of the courtyard in the fortress of Antonia in which Jesus waited to be judged by Pilate. The discoveries of the Dead Sea manuscripts are another example.

On the other hand, other branches of history and archaeology can throw light on parts of the Bible; Egyptology provides information in connection with the episodes of Joseph and Moses, and we turn to Mesopotamian archaeology in order to gain a better idea of Abraham and the deportation of the Chosen People to Babylon by Nabuchodonosor. The four hundred years preceding the birth of Christ could only be studied in the Bible—which has little to say about them—by reference to Greek and Roman history; but now the discovery of the spiritual treasures of the Essenes in the Dead Sea caves has thrown new light on these last centuries of the Jewish community.

The result of all this work has been summarized by Sir Charles Marston in the title of his book *The Bible is True*.[1] Not everything in this book can be accepted without reserve, but in its general intention it remains valuable. We see that the sacred text is a document as worthy of interest and study as the various chronicles and histories bequeathed to us by the other peoples of antiquity. There can be no doubt that it is this fact, daily becoming clearer, that largely explains the interest shown in the Bible by people today.

HOW HISTORY THROWS LIGHT ON THE SACRED TEXT

The contribution made by the historical study of the Bible to the knowledge and comprehension of the sacred text is so immense that we can do no more here than give a few brief illustrations. Various precise details, customs and even proper

[1] *The Bible is True. The lessons of the 1925–1934 excavations in Bible lands summarized and explained* (London, 1934).

names which could formerly be regarded as legendary now reappear against a clearly defined historical background. For example, when we found Abraham buying from a Hittite king the cave of Machpelah to bury his wife in, or when Uriah, the unfortunate husband of Bathsheba, the victim of King David's criminal adultery, was described as a Hittite, the term meant nothing until Perrot's first investigations, Winckler's excavations at Boghaz-Keui and Hrozny's decipherment of the tablets discovered there revealed the great destiny of this Hittite people which for nearly five centuries dominated Asia Minor and its approaches. Those famous Philistines whom Samson fought so joyfully are emerging into the light of history now that it seems almost certain that they are to be connected with the first waves of the Aryan invasion; scenes, painted in the time of Ramesses III, of the invasion of the "Sea Peoples" have been found in the Valley of Kings, and Mycenae and Tiryns have shown us fortresses similar to those that Josue and his successors had to attack. Goliath, the tall, blond Aryan, may be a cousin of Homer's Hector.

Certain customs which, in the Bible, might seem strange or even shocking, are confirmed and illuminated by history and its auxiliary, archaeology. An episode like Abraham sacrificing Isaac, which implies the existence of human sacrifice, has become much more comprehensible since, in the tombs of Chaldaea and on the high places of Palestine, skeletons have been found which are clearly those of children and servants put to death as a sacrifice. As for the famous "ram caught in a thicket" which the Angel of the Lord substituted for young Isaac, a perfectly identifiable statue of it has been found at Ur. The vow of *herem* or anathema, that is, total destruction of a captured city, astonishing as such an act may appear when carried out by poverty-stricken tribes who must have delighted in their conquests, can henceforth be seen to derive from a ritual of immemorial antiquity that was followed everywhere. In the foundations of Jericho the marks of a fire have been found; perhaps it was the one started by Josue.

More generally, we find that certain important episodes in

the Bible, when placed in the political and psychological context of their age, acquire in this new light a sort of unexpected
depth. The departure of Abraham and his clan from Ur of the
Chaldees for Palestine can be understood from a psychological
point of view which recent events in the modern world help us
to grasp. Supposing a species of polytheistic totalitarian dic-
tatorship had been imposed on Mesopotamia, with all the
minutely detailed regulations revealed in the Babylonian codes
of law, it would be natural for the monotheist Abraham to want
to escape by "choosing liberty"; the voice of God and the voice
of his own conscience were at one: an attractive lesson, that has
much to teach us.

It is impossible to understand without reference to historical
events the amazing change in the attitude of the Pharaoh to be
observed at the beginning of the story of Moses. In the previous
chapter Joseph, as vizier of the Egyptian monarch, has obtained
for his brothers the right to settle in the land of Gessen, not far
from the Delta; we turn the page and what do we find? Persecution, the Hebrews subjected to forced labour and the massacre of their new-born children. What has happened? History
provides the answer by telling us about the invasion of the
Hyksos or Shepherd Kings, Semitic in origin, who occupied the
land of the Nile for more than a century. The Pharaoh who
appointed Joseph as his chief minister was probably a Hyksos.
The Hebrews were cousins of these invaders and worked with
them. As a result, when the "leprosy of Asia" had been ejected
by the nationalist movement led by the priests of Thebes, they
found themselves treated, as collaborators of the occupiers,
with the severity of which we read.

If we continue to follow the course of events in the Bible, we
find the explanation of another mystery. Josue and his bands
attack the land of Canaan and encounter a great many difficulties; they need no less than two or three miracles from Yahweh
to enable them to gain a foothold. After all, they can only have
been a wretched troop of bedouins, with no military equipment,
mediocre weapons and few fighting men. How did these
wretched invaders manage, in a mere hundred years, to gain

possession of Palestine? If we notice that these events were taking place at the end of the twelfth century before our era, and if we remember that at the same time the Aryan invasion was in full flood, the explanation seems to be clear. The on-slaught of the invaders forces the great empires to withdraw the garrisons they maintained in colonial regions; Palestine has no more Egyptian, Mesopotamian or Hittite occupiers, but only native kinglets and princelings. But for this providential event, it seems unlikely that the Judges would have succeeded in their enterprises of conquest.

Even the early chapters of Scripture, those of Genesis, so long regarded by freethinkers as legend pure and simple, have been illuminated in recent times by archaeological evidence. We now know that these ancient stories, collected by Jewish tradition, are closely bound up with the civilization that Abraham knew; that we must go back to at least 3000 B.C. to find the cultural context of the story of the creation of man; that the biblical Flood is obviously the monotheistic version of an account of the same event which occurs in the polytheistic epic of Gilgamesh; that the excavations at Kish have even revealed the occurrence of a deluge of catastrophic proportions at a time when there was already a civilization on the Euphrates; and that the Tower of Babel shows a remarkable likeness to the "Ziggurats", the terraced towers of the Mesopotamian religion of the stars, which the Hebrew monotheists naturally saw as symbols of the mad pride of man, who makes himself idols with his own hands instead of giving himself to the one and only true God.

INFLUENCES ON THE BIBLE?

This historical and archaeological investigation of the Bible does more than illuminate and buttress its text. It would be absurd to hide the fact that it also discloses what Mgr Weber calls "resemblances in composition between the Bible and neighbouring literatures". In some cases it is a question not only of literary but also of factual and doctrinal similarities;

for example, after the sojourn in Egypt the Hebrew people adopted a clerical organization, unknown to its ancestors in the desert, which it had been able to observe at close quarters within the extremely clerical borders of the land of the Pharaohs. Similarly there can be no doubt that the importance assumed by the cult of angels owed something to the "cherubim" of Mesopotamia and also to the celestial beings of Persian tradition. There is no need to be amazed or scandalized at this if we remember the exact definition of the divine inspiration of the Bible; if God made use of men, why should they not have been sensitive to human influences, as we all are?

In some cases the resemblance between the biblical text and these "sources" is so marked that people have sometimes wondered if the inspired author used a pagan model, or if the two texts, the pagan and the inspired, were based on a single source. This is particularly striking in the case of Genesis and especially of the Flood, which is one of the outstanding features of the whole Mesopotamian tradition. The code of Hammurabi, which can be seen at the Louvre, a handsome black slab on which this Babylonian king of the beginning of the second millennium engraved his collected laws, contains ordinances similar to those of Moses. Moreover the Mosaic laws also bear resemblances to the commandments to be read in the Book of the Dead from ancient Egypt. The Song of Songs is related to some wedding hymns found on the banks of the Nile, and the compiler of the section of the book of Proverbs (22–4) often called "Sayings of the wise men" may have been influenced by the Egyptian sage Amenemope or have influenced the latter himself. The same problem of attribution arises with regard to Psalm 104, which is almost modelled on the hymn composed in honour of his only God, the Sun, by the interesting revolutionary Pharaoh Amenophis IV, also known as Akhenaton; unless it was the biblical text that influenced the Egyptian. The Greek book of Wisdom employs the vocabulary of the Alexandrian philosophers and to some extent reflects their doctrines. This kind of resemblance can be discovered even in the Gospel;

Dioscurides'[1] treatise on medicine had been so well studied by the doctor Luke that when the latter came to write his Gospel he more or less borrowed his opening sentences from Dioscurides.

To all of which should be added, in Mgr Weber's words:

> To avoid any scandal that might be caused by these remarks, it should be emphasized that these comparisons, which shed a powerful light on the biblical texts and enable us to understand them, also throw into relief the profoundly human and at the same time transcendental character of the sacred books; for nowhere do we find what often disfigures ancient works: complicated and extravagant notions, immorality or at least sensuality, and above all the polytheism or at any rate pantheism in which pagan documents are literally drenched. *Yet* [our italics] *our Jewish or Christian books are the product of a people at a far lower stage of cultural development than the empires which dominated the Near East in the centuries before Christ, or than Greek circles.*

In this essential difference we can see the whole point of these comparisons and of the search for resemblances; we can see the transcendence of a will that gives history its whole meaning and import.

THE LIMITS OF HISTORY

For indispensable as it is to fix the Bible properly on its foundations and defend it against adversaries who can see nothing but myth in it, and to study the sacred text in accordance with history, it would nevertheless be a grave mistake to stop there. The most precise—and the most pious—of "sacred histories" would still be only an introduction to the study of the Bible. That is why, together with the historical approach, another approach must be—and in fact is being—employed; its aim is to explain and deepen the permanent religious value of Scripture. Gripping and illuminating as it often is, historical

---

[1] A Greek who served as a doctor in the Roman army and probably wrote his *Materia Medica* in the reign of Nero. [*Trans.*]

research must not make us lose sight of the real goal. Study of the political, archaeological, sociological and literary factors which constitute the human framework of Revelation must in no wise remain an end in itself. The ultimate goal is to hear the Word of God, to understand that his will is at work among men and rules the fate of worlds. We can never attain to a full understanding of the Bible unless we really believe that it contains the Message of Life, that it is, above all, the Book of the Acts of God.

CHAPTER VII

THE BOOK OF THE ACTS
OF GOD

GOD ACTS IN HISTORY

The expression "Acts of God" must be understood in both senses of the word "act", that is, legal document and action. As an inspired book, the Bible is the expression of the Word; but it is something else as well: the manifestation of God in deeds. All through Scripture the Lord speaks, but he also acts, and this action is no less revealing for man, no less exemplary and formative. No doubt the whole of human history, "that long chain of the immediate causes that make and unmake empires", as Bossuet[1] says, "is dependent on the secret orders of Providence", but the formal and very precise plan of the Bible is to show men explicitly that "their whole history, everything that happened to them from day to day, was only a continual fulfilment of the oracles delivered to them by the Holy Spirit". The lesson repeated over and over again in the books of the Bible—unlike the one suggested by Greco-Roman paganism—is that man, in the events of history, is not the plaything of a blind fate but in the hands of a Power, a Principle, a personal God on whom all depends and who wishes to lead him to his true goal.

That is what gives the Bible its very special meaning and

[1] This famous seventeenth-century bishop was tutor to Louis XIV's son, and wrote, primarily for his pupil's benefit, a *Discourse on Universal History.* [*Trans.*]

what was already known by its inspired authors, who, in all they wrote, had but one purpose: to bring home to men the action of God in the world and in the dimension of time. To reproach them with lack of the famous modern "objectivity" is pointless. For them, history is written at God's dictation as part of his designs: the moral writings seek to elevate man to the likeness of God; poetry in its various forms exalts the glory of the Most High and furnishes believers with the means of associating themselves with his work through prayer; and the *midrashim*[1] bring home the infallibility of his actions.

What gives the historical study of the Bible its whole import and puts the Bible as a history book in a class by itself is that this slice of events cut out of time and space reveals the divine action; in fact, it is the divine action, directed towards Revelation. An indissoluble union of human realities—some of them a painful, even a lamentable sight—and transcendent and divine realities; that is the very substance of the Bible; that is what constitutes its greatness, but also its difficulty.

THE PROBLEM OF MIRACLES

God's action has on occasion taken the form of direct, outward, perceptible interventions called miracles. The Council of Trent described them as "arguments demonstrating the infinite omnipotence of God and also sure signs, suited to all intelligences, of the divine Revelation". For a believing Christian it is obvious that there can be no question of denying the reality of the miracles reported in the Bible. From the moment we assume that God created and controls the world it becomes perfectly comprehensible that he should produce symbolic manifestations of the supernatural efficacy of his action in deeds, matter and bodies. A miracle is simply a perceptible token of the Revelation contained in the Bible as a whole.

Nevertheless it would be futile to deny that for modern minds, conditioned, sometimes unconsciously, by an atmosphere of rationalism and often sordid realism, miracles constitute a stumbling block. As Mgr Mignot wrote half a century

[1] For the meaning of this term, see above, p. 51.

ago: "At the present time miracles are for many people an obstacle rather than a road to belief. The modern mind, fashioned in the so-called scientific mould, is ill at ease when confronted with a miracle. Even in those not frightened by the supernatural there is a hint of embarrassment, of hesitation, of uncertainty, of doubt."[1] How is this difficulty, which clearly does exist, to be met today by the reader of the Bible, who enjoys the benefit of papal teaching and the illumination of the numerous commentaries on the subject?

First, in accordance with the invitation of *Divino afflante Spiritu*, he will take into account the existence of different "literary *genres*", that is to say, he will put the provisional question whether the biblical writer, when he reported something extraordinary or supernatural, wished to present it as a historical fact. The *midrash* of Jonas or the epic poem about Josue's mighty deed are obviously not written in the same register as the chapters in the Gospels which tell us of Christ's Resurrection; the credence given to this last event is not of the same order as that accorded to the stopping of the sun or the swallowing of the prophet by the sea monster.

As for the miraculous incidents which figure in the strictly historical books, they can be placed in three categories. Some look simply providential; others consist in a concatenation of apparently natural events whose mere accumulation seems to proceed from a divine intention; and the rest, which show God's direct action thwarting or replacing an apparently natural cause, are more precisely miracles in the full sense of the term. With regard to the incidents in the first two categories, we must look at them objectively without overestimating (or underestimating) their marvellous character. Some of them can even be placed in a basically natural context; the supernatural factor is then their occurrence in conditions reported by the Bible and reflecting God's will. For example, the crossing of the Red Sea by the Hebrews under Moses has been connected with the peculiar behaviour of the tides in the Elamitic gulf, and

---

[1] *Lettres sur les études ecclésiastiques*, p. 119.

manna with a white truffle found in the Arabian desert or the sugary gum produced by certain acacias; but that does not alter the fact that in saving his people from massacre or hunger the Almighty was carrying out an intention, a plan that transcends any down-to-earth "scientific" explanation. Similarly it has been possible to make a list of the "ten plagues of Egypt" from documents found in the country itself and from observation of its geography, climate and fauna; but the simultaneous apparition of these phenomena, their extraordinarily widespread character, the enormous assistance they gave to the chosen people and the results they achieved obviously prove that they were willed by God.

The will of God is still more evident in the case of miracles which cannot be connected with any natural cause, especially those we see performed—forty-one times during the course of his life on earth—by Jesus, which impress themselves on our minds as the indubitable expression of the divine action by their sublime simplicity, their infinite charity and the lessons they teach. Confronted with incidents like the curing of the paralytic or the raising of Lazarus, vouched for as true by the Gospel, we must either recognize God's will at work or else reject the Gospel, the complete Christian revelation and religion as a whole. That is what St Thomas Aquinas meant when he laid much more emphasis on miracles as "signs of faith" than as proofs of faith.[1]

[1] In the *Summa Theologica*, II, II, Q. 178, art. 1, we find several passages in which this idea is formulated: St Thomas declared that "miracles are called signs because they are manifestations of a supernatural reality, an exceptional intervention by God".

Miracles are the *effect of faith*, whether it be the faith of him who performs them or the faith of those for whom they are performed. St Thomas quotes the words of St Matthew (13. 58): "Nor did he do many miracles there [i.e. Nazareth], because of their unbelief." Yet St Thomas says miracles serve to confirm faith, not as a proof of faith, but by causing the performance of the acts of faith which develop this virtue: "just as it is not sufficient to receive the grace of faith, but also necessary to have the grace to hear the teaching which instructs faith, so the performance of miracles is necessary for the confirmation of faith" (art. 5)

EVENTS AS ACTS OF GOD

But it is not by the miracles alone—far from it—that the Bible makes God's action apparent. It would be stupid to let oneself be in any way fascinated by these extraordinary incidents to the extent of being prevented from discerning something far vaster, God's actual plan, of which the miracles are simply exceptional evidence; the sign would then be deflecting us from the reality it denotes. We must recognize God's action from one end of Scripture to the other; it is present in men's minds as well as in events, gently leading humanity little by little to greater enlightenment, making it follow, painfully no doubt, but providentially, that ascending curve that we must trace through the Bible if we wish to understand the sometimes disconcerting succession of its heterogeneous books.

The Bible in its two parts, which are tightly bound together and dependent on each other, is the account—an incomplete one, no doubt, for there are gaps in it, but a perfectly coherent one—of God's activity in the world, right from the start up to the moment when, with the last of the Apostles about to disappear from the scene, the message of Revelation was entrusted to the Church of Christ; it is also, from the Creation described in Genesis to the Last Judgement symbolically presented in the Apocalypse, the complete history of humanity in the hand of God.

This history has a meaning, it obeys an intention; a meaning and intention discerned by Christians and identified in their eyes with the mystery of the Incarnation. There is Pascal's well-known aphorism: "Jesus Christ, whom both Testaments look to, the Old as its hope, the New as its model, both as their centre" (*Pensées*, 740). The aphorism has a double meaning; Christ is "the centre of the Scriptures" or, if you prefer, their attained goal, because his teaching crowns the whole teaching of the Bible; but, historically speaking, he is the secret thread which binds together all the events. We do not understand a word of the Bible if we are not conscious the whole time of the double fact, primary in its importance, of the Incarnation of the Word and the Redemption by the Cross. Christ is foretold not only by the Prophets and all the inspired passages in which his coming can be traced, but also by the very facts of history, the first clear signs of the divine purpose, from which was deduced, by the light of the Holy Spirit, the divine truth. Abraham's call, the crossing of the Red Sea, the creation of the Davidic kingdom, the deportation to Babylon, the revolt of the Machabees; all these events and many others can only be understood by reference to the coming of Christ. Symbolically they foretell it, historically they prepare the political, psychological, social and above all religious climate which was to enable the second Person of the Trinity to bring his message to humanity, and Christianity to triumph because it fulfilled a long-felt hope.

THE MYSTERY OF ISRAEL

It is impossible to consider God's purpose made manifest in events without coming upon a historical mystery, the mystery of Israel. As human author of the Bible, the Hebrew people asserts that it is in receipt of spiritual assistance, inspiration; as an actor in biblical events, it declares that it enjoys God's special protection, the Covenant. To what extent does a historical view of the facts corroborate these two assertions?

From the purely literary point of view, there is a problem which is insoluble if we rule out divine intervention; how was this people without arts, philosophy and any particular natural endowments able to produce this incomparable masterpiece, while people infinitely more advanced intellectually have left books full of gross moral and religious errors?

From the strictly historical point of view, how was this tiny people—in the time of Solomon's splendour it never exceeded a million souls—able to exert such widespread influence? Persecuted, tortured, reduced in the dark days of the captivity "by the waters of Babylon" to less than a hundred thousand exiles, how was it able to survive right up to the present day, while the mighty empires all round it have left us only ruins, inscriptions and mummies? And why did the long trial which was its destiny lead it step by step, from suffering to suffering, ever upwards towards the Revelation?

This mystery of Israel is so closely bound up with the deep meaning of the Bible that we are brought up against it just when we discover, in the Incarnation, the final significance of all the events of Scripture. To the question why the chosen people, which had brought forth the Messias and long been big with hope of him, refused him when he came, there is no answer but a supernatural one. The human reasons that Israel had for rejecting Jesus, if they do not excuse the wickedness of Calvary, at any rate allow us to understand the drama. Was a people which had had to struggle for generations against neighbours and oppressors, in whom it recognized enemies of its faith, ready to hear the universalist message of Jesus? Could a people whose religious leaders had obstinately taught strict observance of the letter of the law hear without anger that "the letter kills and the spirit alone makes us free"? Could a people which for centuries had expected a glorious Messias, who would restore its power and sovereignty, recognize this ineffable figure in the child of a carpenter of Nazareth, in an artisan surrounded by Galilean fishermen? But if we think of what was to be the terribly logical consequence of this quite comprehensible attitude, if we believe that the sacrifice of Calvary was necessary to the work of salvation—*sine sanguine non fit remissio*—are we not brought face to face with a decisive mystery? Even in its refusal Israel remains the instrument of God.

THE POTTER'S WORK

There is another divine purpose which can be traced from one end of the Bible to the other, inseparably united to that revealed in the march of events; it is the work of the perfecting of man, and it is essential to understand it properly if we do not want to encounter a serious difficulty: the apparent difference between the religion of the Old Testament and that of the New. Only the idea of guided development, of progressive enlightenment with a full revelation at the end of it, enables us to resolve contradictions which would otherwise give scandal.

Very often the Bible compares God to a potter modelling human clay; "As clay in the hand of the potter", says Jeremias, "so are men in the hand of God" (Jer. 18. 6). Scripture is thus the story of this progressive refinement, of this patient work by the Creator on his creature to bring him to greater perfection. And just as a potter does not transform the lump of clay that he is modelling into a vase with skilful curves instantaneously, so God reveals himself at work throughout the Bible and seems to enjoy displaying his alterations, his momentary defeats, his regrets and his fresh starts.

That is perhaps the most exhilarating aspect of the Bible; it gives a constant sense of progress. "The historian receives an extraordinary impression from the Bible," writes Fr de Lubac.[1] "The contrast between the humbleness of Israel's beginnings and the power of the seeds—explosives would be a better term —it bears within itself; the concrete and at first somewhat veiled form taken by its highest beliefs; then the majestic progress, the confident if mysterious march towards something vast and unforeseeable; nowhere else do we find anything even remotely resembling all this."

The truth that brings perfection and salvation was certainly not revealed complete by God at one blow; the clay did not receive its final beauty from the potter right from the start. All through Israel's history we have to note an ascent towards the Light, a slow advance in knowledge of the unutterable. To be sure, it was an ascent and advance that was constantly compromised and threatened, for it was made by men like ourselves, a prey to temptation and sin; but the miseries on which the biblical writers never hesitate to cast a harsh light, far from harming the truth of the picture as a whole, only reinforce it, just as virtue always looks more admirable when it blossoms

[1] Catholicisme, les aspects sociaux du dogme, by Henri de Lubac, S.J. (4th revised edn., Paris, 1947), p. 131. English Trans.: Catholicism, A study of Dogma in Relation to the Corporate Destiny of Mankind, translated by Lancelot C. Sheppard (London, 1950), p. 81.

next to vice. The great principle dominating the composition of Scripture is that of the ascent towards total discovery. This ascent is divided into three stages: Abraham receives the revelation of the unity of God; Moses, on Sinai, writes, at the dictation of the Almighty, the religious and moral law which is to rule the life of the chosen people; and finally the prophets contribute to a transference of religion from the realm of sociology, where loyalty to the sacred precepts is confused with membership of the chosen people, to within the individual, where each one is responsible for his own acts alone, for all his acts, according to the voice of conscience and under the gaze of God.

We have only to read the Old Testament to feel an urgent demand arising in our minds. These three stages are still only a preparation. We expect something else: a religion in which the whole of nature will be consecrated, divinized, in which the human condition itself will be assumed by the light that is life. "Christ has superseded the law", says St Paul (Rom. 10. 4), and the Epistle to the Hebrews states exactly how: "In old days, God spoke to our fathers in many ways and by many means, through the prophets; now at last in these times he has spoken to us, with a Son to speak for him" (Heb. 1. 1–2). What astonishes and sometimes shocks us in the religion of the Old Testament is only preparation and tentative essay, but everything contributes to a fulfilment whose other name is Revelation. All the great doctrinal themes of the Bible necessarily end in the Gospel; all the truths it communicates to men only disclose their full meaning in the light shed by the latter; and it is given to us to know the accents, the living Incarnation of the Word which God progressively allowed men to hear. Jesus is the form willed by the potter.

CHAPTER VIII

THE OLD TESTAMENT, THE
BOOK OF PREPARATION

THE TRADITION OF THE CREATION

The Old Testament recounts the first part of this sacred history. In its forty-five books it groups together everything preceding the coming of Christ.

It begins with a series of mysterious writings, bearing the title of Genesis, about the origin of the world and of man. They are among the most famous parts of the whole Bible, the parts which can be alluded to in anyone's presence without fear of incomprehension. How God made heaven and earth, how he modelled the first man from the primeval mud, and how, from this first living flesh of the male man—such is perhaps the meaning of the Sumerian syllable *ti*, which is also translated by "rib"—he drew the female; all these episodes form such an integral part of elementary education that it is impossible to imagine our civilization being unaware of them. They are immemorial traditions, bequeathed to the Hebrews by peoples who lived long before them. In the black tent by Mambre,[1] then in the little white houses of the Delta, the bards would intone them in the evenings, long chants in the oriental style, tales heard a hundred times yet always new. So, later, in Mycenaean fortresses, other poets would tirelessly recite the story of their great elders who went off to Troy to win back Helen and had many an adventure on their homeward journey.

[1] Mam(b)re in Canaan could be seen from the field where Abraham buried Sara (Gen. 23.19). [*Trans.*]

In the first eleven chapters of Genesis the revealed truth which is their basis thus rubs shoulders with popular tradition and also the thunder and lightning of an apocalyptic proclamation. In many respects the pages depicting the archangel with a fiery sword barring man from Paradise and the wrath of the Lord submerging guilty humanity under a terrifying waste of waters correspond to those in the last book of Scripture which were to portray the end of the world; a mysterious and significant connection. But what is especially admirable in these eleven chapters is their psychological profundity and their religious truth. Christian morality sprang from them; the picture that thousands of human beings have formed and still form of their destiny, the explanation of our inward misery, the hope that buoys us up, all the most decisive elements in us are the product of these pages. Above all, there is the great certainty of faith, the truth which was to be passed on right through the Bible down to us: there is only one God and everything in the world obeys his Law. The exacting and uncompromising monotheism of these pages is enough to differentiate them radically from the other cosmogonies of neighbouring peoples, with which they have been expressly compared.

Right from the start this testimony is declared to have been given by one people—one family, one line of descent. The link is expressly indicated. The Book of Genesis does not end—far from it—with the story of the flood and the drama of the tower of Babel, a prelude to the great divisions of humanity; a genealogy follows immediately, one of those long lists of names which occur frequently in the Bible and were considered enormously important by the Hebrews, as they were by all the peoples of the East. From the first man to the first witness of the revelation—and right down past him to Jesus—the line is direct, precise and clearly traced. That means that between the message of salvation and those immemorial traditions there is a close link; the one depends on the other. Those sublime myths are already the truth and the life; they are already the revelation.

THE AGE OF THE PATRIARCHS

However, the revelation began formally on the day when a nomadic Semite in the neighbourhood of Ur of the Chaldees heard an ineffable call and obeyed the supernatural command. What call? The call of the one god, the true god, of God. He whom the human spirit discovers, but can only know darkly, selected Abraham, son of Terah, as the messenger of his Word and ordered him to break with the errors and abominations of polytheism. We are confronted here with an essentially mystical and inexplicable fact, as mysterious in its essence and as tangible in its results as the mission of Joan of Arc, perhaps, for France. How, why, in a world soaked in idolatry, did a small bedouin clan, led by its chief, opt for the truth? The answer is obviously to be found in the will of God, already at work.

From the moment the Voice resounded, men were therefore face to face with the truth and their duty was to serve it. In this sense—a sense often recalled by our medieval sculptors—the whole of humanity, when it is faithful to the truth, is the child of Abraham. But will it be faithful? This question, which always arises, arose right at the beginning of the story. Abraham went off with his clan, leaving the pagan city, marching into the desert. Did he know, at the bottom of his heart, that his unprecedented decision was opening a new chapter in history, that until the end of time it was going to pose to the human conscience "the one and only problem"? He himself, like all those who dare to take great spiritual risks, had his doubts. Would the God who had summoned him continue to support him? Would he appear before him again to help and guide him? Yes; and it was on an evening when he felt discouraged and, as an act of faith, offered a sacrifice that he received the reply. God was present. God spoke; he granted his Covenant to his servant and to all his descendants. A contract was drawn up; the people later to be called Israel, Abraham's posterity, was to enjoy the distinction of special protection, it was to be the chosen people, as long as it remained faithful, carried out the Lord's commands and was the depository of the great truth of the One God.

Henceforth everything was to fall into place with remorseless logic. Sarah, Abraham's wife, had no children. Would God fail to keep his word? What was the point of the Covenant if the contracting party had no issue? The miracle took place; the old woman brought forth a child and was so delighted that he was called Isaac, that is to say, "son of joy." Yet God seemed to remain silent, or rather his will was not clear. What did he really want? Abraham believed that he expected the hardest sacrifice, that of this first child. There was nothing for it but to obey, hard as it might be to do so. On the high place the sacrificial knife was about to pierce Isaac's throat when the Angel of the Lord held back the father's hand and pointed to the ram that was to be substituted for the human victim. "I prefer obedience to sacrifice", a prophet was to say later; the lesson had already been given on Mount Moriah.

Faithfulness, obedience; but what else exactly did God want? Slowly, gropingly as it were, Abraham's descendants sought the answer, through episodes rich in symbols. Isaac's marriage signified that the clan of Terah was to remain pure and not mix its blood with any other; Jacob, "wrestling with an angel" for a whole night by the River Jabbok, was obliged to come to grips with his human condition, and choose between the flesh and the spirit, personal interest and his vocation.

Soon the whole people was confronted by this problem. In Egypt, where famine led them and Joseph settled them, Abraham's descendants perhaps thought that surrounded by idols with animals' faces they would easily be able to preserve their faith. The answer they received was persecution, suffering and anguish. Obeying God is not easy. But the seal put on his people by the Lord genuinely protected it. How many centuries of slavery were there? Two or three at least; but there was enough loyalty and courage left in Israel's soul for faith to survive the test. The first stage ends with the book of Genesis, the stage in which this still elementary but solid faith is proclaimed; the second is about to begin.

GOD'S LAWGIVER

Moses is so important that the Bible devotes no less than four books to him. Exodus tells above all the story of the origin of his mission and of his work until he draws near to the land which God had promised his people; it also describes many rules and ordinances fixed by God's great lawgiver. Leviticus consists almost entirely of a code of laws and collection of rites. With Numbers the narrative is resumed and shows the chosen people on the march towards the spot assigned by Providence. Finally, Deuteronomy is in some sort a spiritual testament of the great leader; his last instructions are noted with burning devotion, and we can almost hear the lawgiver's actual voice begging his people never to betray the law he has revealed to it.

That is Moses' true mission, his supernatural rôle, the one assigned to him when, already advanced in age—he was to die forty years later aged 120—a shepherd on the slopes of Madian, he heard God's voice in the burning bush calling him to action. There is scarcely a difficulty that he did not encounter. His first task was to snatch his people from slavery, and for that nothing less was required than the miraculous intervention of God, who smote the persecutors with the "ten plagues" and drowned their army in the Red Sea's swift returning waters. Then he had to combat the lack of understanding, the selfishness, the low passions—in a word, the call of the flesh—which urged the chosen nation to revolt and, at their leader's first absence, hurled it back into idolatry. But no matter; by his iron will, by his genius and with God's help, Moses was to force on this "stiff-necked people" the truth received on Sinai. The Tables of the Law, the Ten Commandments; those were the bases of the morality given by God's witness to his people and, beyond it, to the whole of humanity. And if this people needed forty years to accept them, the desert was there to provide an appropriate background to the trial.

So forty years went by. All the adults died, and Moses himself, too; for once doubting God and his power he was not to see the crowning of his work. But out of that horde of fugitives he had made a nation; and he had given it a constitution founded on the Ten Commandments which was to last for centuries. The second stage in the spiritual pilgrimage was over. "The one and only God," said Abraham; "and the Law", added Moses.

THE JUDGES AND KINGS

Now we have emerged into history, a history, it is true, still close to the popular chronicle and at the same time full of meaning. Israel now stands before the land pointed out by God as the fore-ordained scene of the fulfilment of its destiny. This land has first to be occupied, then, after the conquest, settled and organized. That is, some kind of government has to be set up, for it is obvious that a settled, agricultural nation cannot be ruled in the same way as clans of pastoral nomads. But immediately a serious problem arises, the problem that arises for all men as soon as they have begun to own property, land and wealth. In the poverty and homelessness of the desert God was near and loyalty relatively easy; will it be so easy when money and commerce have exercised their pernicious influence on Israel's soul? Will not God then abandon his people?

That is the great debate that goes on through the six books, at first sight purely historical, known as Josue, Judges, Samuel (two books that really form one) and Kings (again two consecutive books). Josue, Moses' successor, assisted by the Almighty, leads the chosen people to the conquest of the Promised Land. It is not an easy conquest, in spite of favourable historical circumstances, but it is brought to a successful conclusion and the Israelite nation is henceforth mistress of its fate. When a threat arises on the twelve tribes' vague frontiers or in that inner domain which is religion, God raises up a herald to wear his sword and preach his word, the "Judge" who commands in battle or reigns in peace. Thus it is a broken piecemeal history, darting its attention from one corner of Palestine to the other, and leaving the impression of an unstable and precarious government.

After two centuries the people begins to feel keenly the worry of this instability and wonders why it cannot have a single leader like its cousins, a king to assure its unity. The national assembly votes for this solution and Saul, apparently singled out by God for the part, is about to be crowned. But at this point a problem is raised by Samuel, the old seer, the sage whose task it is to anoint with holy oil the forehead, shoulders and chest of the king-elect. He puts the people on its guard. Israel is adopting the customs of others, but Israel is not like other peoples. The monarchy will perhaps be its temporal salvation, but what of its spiritual salvation?

In the event Samuel's prediction comes true. From the temporal point of view, in spite of severe crises threatening the country's unity at the accession of King David, afterwards, during the reign of his son Solomon, the arrangement is a success. But oppression soon sets in; the most ostentatious sovereigns are also those that cost their subjects the most trouble. From the spiritual point of view the outlook is still worse. Even David, devoted to God and mystical psalmist though he was, seriously disobeyed the divine law; Solomon's thousand wives find it only too easy to sap his loyalty to God. It looks as though the price of Israel's glory and earthly success will be the loss of its ideal and whole reason for existence. The Baals and Astartes worshipped just outside the shining temple of the One God are bound to draw down the wrath of heaven on the sinning capital, Jerusalem.

The drama has begun. Rent asunder into two hostile parts, the kingdom of Solomon rushes headlong to destruction; the trial is to teach Israel Yahweh's lesson. Slowly and patiently the Justice that none escapes draws nigh; two hundred years pass before it overtakes the northern kingdom, the one whose capital is Samaria, and three hundred and fifty before it overtakes the southern kingdom, Judah and Jerusalem. The spiritual treason becomes more blatant; the kings think only of negotiating fruitful alliances with the pagans; they adopt their gods and abominable customs; and in the centre of Jerusalem children are sacrificed to Baal, as they are in Phoenicia. But only patience is needed; God's wrath is at work. The Assyrians and, after them, Nebuchodonosor's mercenaries are his instruments. Mangled, tortured, deported, the descendants of Abraham and the kings at last see their fault. "Out of the depths have I cried unto thee, O Lord; Lord, hear my voice. O let thine ears consider well the voice of my supplication."

THE MESSAGE OF THE PROPHETS

God was not silent all through this drama. He still spoke to his people through the voices of his prophets; and the Bible brings us their words in four books, one for Isaias, one for Jeremias, one for Ezechiel and one for the "twelve minor prophets", so called not because their message is less important, but because it is reported in fewer words. These mouthpieces of the Almighty differ in social origin, style and temperament, but taken as a whole they have the same character. Commissioned by God with the superhuman task of recalling the chosen people to obedience, they carry out their mission to the end without fear or hesitation; their lives are less important to them than the message they bear. It was they who finally saved faith, principles and hope. "Springs of living water in the middle of an arid desert," Mgr Ricciotti calls them, "men of providence whose teaching enabled Israel's soul to climb to the third stage in its spiritual ascent."

The first of them are in action in the time of the kings; Osee and Amos fighting with all their strength against the abuses of their time; Micheas, when Samaria fell, pointing out the consequences but already proclaiming the hope he sees in the future; Nahum recognizing and acclaiming in the fall of Nineveh God's sovereign action in the world; Abdias exalting his people's vocation in terms of a narrow nationalism.

The book bearing the name of Isaias, the greatest genius in

this whole amazing band of seers, spans the years from the age of Achaz and Ezechias to that of the Babylonian exile, such a lengthy period that scholars have long wondered if there were not in fact two, or perhaps even three, writers involved. Yet, in spite of variations in the style, the book as a whole forms a unity because of the messianic idea which inspires it from start to finish and provides the prophet with his most moving words. The promise of salvation given by Isaias in time of peace is reiterated more fervently in days of suffering and exile. From his text, and especially from the second part (chapter 40 onwards), rises a picture of a regenerate Israel led to salvation by the Messias.

Jeremias is the sorrowful and pathetic witness of the fall of Jerusalem and the temporal collapse of Israel. This drama, which he describes step by step, has its counterpart in his mind, where superhuman hope clashes with human despair, and universal love vies with hatred of infidelity.

Ezechiel, the third of the three "major prophets", who was also a witness of the drama, devotes less time to moral warnings than to the expression of a supernatural hope, formulated in striking terms. Corpses will rise again and flesh once more cover dried bones! So Israel, recalled to life by the Word . . . and so on. This apocalyptic style, dear to latter-day Jewish religious writers, is also the one employed by the book of Daniel. Written in a quite different tone and probably composed of heterogeneous parts, it proclaims this same hope, no longer a temporal one limited to the kingdom of Israel, but reserved for those who live a righteous life, the hope of the kingdom of God.

Thus the prophets play a double rôle: they bring tidings of God's wrath before it is unleashed, but tidings of hope when the wrath has arrived and the people is prostrate and repentant. Then, when the exile is over and Israel has been able to return to its land, the last of them fight the good fight in another way. Aggeus is the champion of the material restoration, the man who demands a temple for the Lord; Zacharias lays more emphasis on the social and political restoration; Joel,[1] concentrating on an eschatological future, exalts the spiritual restoration and sees in penitence the means of retaining God's friendship; Malachias, too, calls for inward reform and proclaims the demands of faith; and in the book of Jonas, inserted among the prophets because the man of this name is a seer belonging to the same intellectual family, although it is only a mere story full of wonders but devoid of oracular pronouncements, there can be heard, like the first echo of Christian universalism, the call to an Israel with a universal mission, summoning all the peoples of the earth to salvation.

THE POST-EXILIC BOOKS

For the exile is over, and the chosen people, thanks to Cyrus' generosity, has been able to settle in Palestine again. But things are not what they were in days gone by, and old men lament the change. The hard toil of the return, the difficulties of restoration, cries of sorrow from those who feel sad when they compare the present with the past; that is what we find to start with in the first of the books constituting the last and extremely heterogeneous part of the Old Testament, Esdras and Nehemias. It was all over; Israel had lost her political freedom for many long centuries. First the Greeks, in the shape of Alexander's heirs, and then the Romans kept the chosen people in varying degrees of subjection. When the tyranny became intolerable, the Machabees organized a national rising. The Bible reports their exploits in two books, the first strictly and movingly historical, the second, it must be admitted, somewhat too much given to edification.

But there was something else to do besides record these glorious but unimportant deeds. While empires, in their rise and fall, unconsciously prepared the world in which the Gospel was to spread and flourish, the little Jewish community, shut in on itself and busily occupied in meditating on the spiritual

[1] It is difficult to give Joel an exact date; the Dominican biblical scholars of Jerusalem make him a contemporary of Osee and Amos.

deposit which it knew very well to be the only reason for its existence, was itself preparing—even to the profound reasons for its refusal—the world in which providence was to make possible the double mystery of the Incarnation and Redemption.

That is the light in which we must look at these post-exilic books in order to understand them; they contain a spiritual message, even those apparently episodic in character. Tobias demonstrates—in rather down-to-earth terms, perhaps—the doctrine of the rewarding of merit by God; Judith is a tale set in cruel times exalting the triumph of faith over human power; Esther is an episode in the lives of the Jews who remained in Persia, proclaiming the same lesson in a different language; Ruth, an exquisite book, on the surface is just an idyll, but it is rich in symbols lovingly used again by Claudel. Ruth's verses seem to point to the messianic horizon; it is placed before the book of Samuel in our Bibles because it introduces us to King David's ancestors.

But these lofty spiritual lessons are given above all by the "sapiential" books, which enlarge and refine them from century to century until they are not far below the level of the Gospel. There is the book of Proverbs, a sort of epitome of ancestral experience, full of aphorisms that have nourished the "wisdom of the nations"; there is Ecclesiastes, with its strong and bitter taste (the famous verse about the vanity of vanities is known to everyone), pointing to virtue as the secret of happiness; there is that mystical masterpiece, the Song of Songs, which, in the classical images of conjugal happiness, tells Israel and, beyond Israel, the human spirit, of the splendour of union with God; there is the book of Job, another masterpiece, not this time of poetry alone, but of dialectic too, probing man's heart and leading him to the calm contemplation of God's plans and mercy; there is Ecclesiasticus, a complete manual of the religious life for anyone wishing to discover the meaning of faith. Last but not least there is the book of Wisdom, which finds the secret of true life in the accomplishment of the divine will and shows that will at work in history. All these books, or at least their final versions, took shape during the last centuries of Israel before Christ. Appearing at a time when the Bible is poor in events they assume the value of evidence; they remind us that true life is not at the mercy of any occupying power but is lived on a plane and aims at a freedom which earthly tyrants are powerless to touch. In this way they foreshadow and prepare us for the message of Christ.

There remains the book of Psalms, which appears in the Bible among the sapiential and poetic books, but occupies a unique position. When were these songs of praise and dedication finally committed to writing? From what more or less ancient sources do the five collections forming the anthology spring? In a way, the answer is of no importance. From David to the sages of the Jewish community after the Exile, what their authors express is so lovely, so pure that the spirit of man will always find refreshment in it. The liturgy of Israel used them; the Christian liturgy knows no finer prayers and lays them under contribution for the bulk of its daily office. Glittering with images and symbols and unfailingly inspired, they are at the same time the literary masterpiece of the whole Old Testament and its spiritual epitome. The spirit of Christ himself was nourished on them and many a time their verses rose to his lips. They are one of the most moving indications of the link between the Old and the New Covenant.

CHAPTER IX

THE NEW TESTAMENT, THE

BOOK OF REVELATION

AN AMAZING STORY

What an admirable and indeed astonishing story it is that fills the chapters of the New Testament! A man appears in the heart of Israel, a distant descendant of King David, but belonging to a humble family, the son of poor people. Long an obscure carpenter in a small village in Galilee, on attaining the age of thirty he "arises", as many prophets have done in days gone by, and travelling right through the Holy Land he speaks, teaches the multitudes and starts a current of opinion. Now this man is much more than a prophet; he is the Messias promised by Scripture; this Son of man is the Son of God. He proves it not only by the miracles he performs, but also by the sublime quality of his teaching. In him are visibly fulfilled Israel's expectation and the hope of the world. An unsurpassable model is set before humanity.

The religious leaders of Israel, however, blinded by their literal interpretation of the old Revelation and perhaps also by extremely temporal considerations, refuse to welcome this new Revelation. Regarded as a false messias, accused of blasphemy and sacrilege, Jesus of Nazareth is arrested, condemned and put to the most shameful and painful of deaths. Is it to be the end of this pitiful story, strikingly like that of many another pseudo-messias thrown up by the age? No. For this man who was defeated—the evidence is plentiful and compels belief—

suddenly triumphs; on the third day after his crucifixion his tomb is found empty, and for close on six weeks in succession he who has risen from the dead appears to one or other of his disciples. By the time he finally quits the scene, in a supreme manifestation of power and glory, those who had followed him and fled like frightened rats at his apparent defeat have regained courage and confidence. Henceforth they will believe and tell the world that the victim of Calvary was in very truth the Messias and the Son of God.

So Christ's first disciples set to work, and their story, as it unfolds, is almost as amazing as their Master's. How was this tiny kernel going to become a tree? How was this sect of poor Jews and Galilean fishermen going, in less than three centuries, to impose itself on the world, penetrate the whole vast Roman empire and substitute its own conception of life for that of ancient paganism? This Revolution of the Cross is itself a mystery. The New Testament describes it, showing the Apostles at the work of proselytizing (they call it evangelization) which will enable the seed sown by Jesus to produce enormous harvests. A new society rises on the foundations laid by him who was crucified at Golgotha, a prefiguration of that city of justice foretold for the end of time by the last book in the Bible.

This sublime story is told in a series of small works which differ considerably in tone but are all extraordinarily rich in texture. The first of them are so pure, so crystalline, that Renan himself called them as a whole "the most beautiful book in the world". Another is a lively and gripping narrative, a sort of adventure story, the story of the early days in the conquest of the world by the cross. Others are doctrinal treatises, the products of particular circumstances, but all sparkling with new ideas which reach right into the dark corners of the soul and force it to aspire to the light. The last is an apocalypse, resembling in form the many conceived by Israel in her last few centuries, but completely Christian in significance. Gospels, Acts of the Apostles, Epistles and Apocalypse; those twenty-seven tiny books contain a message so fresh, so rich and so inexhaustible that in twenty centuries it has lost nothing of its sparkle or topicality.

THE GOSPEL, OR GOOD NEWS

Christ, the living God, is, then, the only subject and the real author of the whole New Testament. The various books only report his life, his message and the circumstances of his appearance for the benefit of his Church after his death. The first part consists of the Gospel, in Greek "the good news", which the herald ran to announce after a military victory. To evangelize was to proclaim this good news, an act which had a venerable and solemn meaning, a religious connotation. For men of Israel, what could this good news be? None other than the news for which they had been hoping for two thousand years: the Messias has come, the kingdom of God is at hand and humanity is going to live under its laws. That is substantially what the Gospel says: Jesus of Nazareth is indeed the expected Messias and the criminal error which put him to death cannot prevail against this certainty; all the rest is only the logical consequence of this affirmation. So the Gospel is at the same time an account of the life, death and resurrection of Jesus and the formulation of the message he brought to the world; the two are identical.

Christ is present in it, a unique model for mankind. It is asserted, and he asserts himself, that he is both man and God. True man, he takes upon himself all the realities of life on earth (evil, from which he is miraculously preserved, is not a positive reality, but an absence), and sanctifies them by the example of his sublime life and death. For the divine is perceptible throughout the Gospel as an ever-present transparent aura which does not affect the genuine, and just as perceptible, humanity of the man-God. United to all men, his brothers, Christ carries them with him up to the supernatural realm where, cleansed of his faults and redeemed, man is more than man; for, true God, he has done all in divine fashion, thus assuring the regeneration of that wretched human nature which he wished to assume for the express purpose of giving man's mortal state its final religious import.

All that in the Old Testament was still only sign, expectation and promise is here accomplished. The Gospel is the climax of the whole Revelation.

THE THREE "SYNOPTIC" GOSPELS

Basically there is only one Gospel. The Good News which Jesus himself is and has brought to the world is handed on in a perfect and definitive form, which may be differently expressed by different books but is substantially one. St Irenaeus aptly speaks of the tetramorphous Gospel, that is, one Gospel with four forms. As early as the end of the second century we find Clement of Alexandria and the Muratorian Canon talking —and it is the only right description—of the Gospel according to St Matthew, according to St Mark, according to St Luke, according to St John, so as to indicate clearly that it is a question of one single set of facts communicated to men with different shades of emphasis.

It might be asked why the Church, when she realized the importance of these writings, did not try to unify them in one narrative. Attempts of this sort were in fact made by several scholars, including the historian Eusebius and, above all, the Syrian Tatian, St Justin's pupil, who did his work very skilfully. They became very popular, but the Church did not set the seal of her approval on them. With her marvellous sense of realities, she probably knew that the tiny differences between the texts, for from prejudicing their credibility, really strengthened it. Above all, with her profound respect for tradition, she did not consider herself entitled to tamper with documents that emanated directly from eye-witnesses.

The resemblances between the first three evangelists, Matthew, Mark and Luke, are particularly striking; many passages in their texts, when placed side by side, look so similar that they are clearly all variants of one single view or, in Greek, *synopsis* of the incident concerned; hence the description of these gospels as synoptic.[1]

They have 350 verses in common, that is, a third of St Matthew (1070) or St. Luke (1151) and more than half St Mark (677). Yet if we compare them with one another we find omissions, additions and differences. Thus St Mark knows nothing of Christ's childhood and omits the Sermon on the Mount, and St Matthew does not report the Ascension; on the other hand, St Luke, in his description of the miraculous birth of Jesus and his early years, is the only one familiar with certain precious details unknown to St Matthew, another authority for the childhood of Christ. Most of the differences are purely formal, but sometimes they look quite serious; for example, in St Matthew and St Luke, when Jesus talks to the apostles before they go off on their mission, he tells them to take nothing with them, "no wallet for the journey, no second coat, no spare shoes *or staff*", whilst in St Mark he recommends them to take "a staff for their journey and nothing more". Such differences prove above all that the Evangelists did not merely copy one another. The resemblances are bound up with the conditions under which the "Synoptics" wrote their books; each of them used the same sources, sometimes studied the books already published by the others and finally made his own personal contribution.

Although they vary in intention and talent from plain popular chronicle to seriously written history, the three Synoptics give one and the same impression. In accordance with a plan which must have been that of the primitive catechism—preaching of St John the Baptist and baptism of Christ, ministry of Jesus in Galilee, journey into Judaea up to Jerusalem, passion, death and resurrection—they retrace the external events of our Lord's life; they report his words as they sounded to his listeners and reflect his attitude with striking exactness; and they are obviously not concerned with scholarly arrangement or theological commentary. They form a record of Christ in three harmonious yet dissimilar parts.

[1] For examples of these similarities, see the end of this book.

THE "JOHANNINE" GROUP

The fourth Gospel, written in his old age by St John, Christ's favourite disciple, the Benjamin of the band of twelve, is quite different. Its differences of form and content were noticed very early on. The author's aim is clearly indicated at the end of his book (20. 31); he wishes to show that Jesus was indeed the Christ, the Son of God, so that all who read may believe in him and thus win salvation. His purpose, then, is apologetic and theological. That does not mean, however, that he does not preserve a very close link between him whom he is the first to call "the Word incarnate" and the actual circumstances of Jesus' life on earth. On the contrary, writing at a time when the three synoptic gospels were already widely read, and assuming the information they impart to be familiar, he provides details forgotten by Matthew, Mark and Luke. It is thanks to him that we know the length of Jesus' public life, the exact date of his death and many circumstances of the Passion. But fundamentally it is not this work of documentation that interests him. The facts are important, but only because of their supernatural significance and the spiritual lessons to be drawn from them. "In the beginning was the Word, and the Word was with God, and the word was God. . . ." We have only to read the first chapter of this book, that sublime passage that Catholics hear, only too often absent-mindedly, at the end of every Mass, to feel that its inspired author was carried aloft as if on wings; the fourth Gospel is the witness of a mystic, the testament of a soul at home with God.

The New Testament canon includes four other books from the same pen as this primary text. There are three letters or Epistles, probably written after the Gospel, the first addressed to a group of Churches in Asia, the second to a "Sovereign Lady" (who was perhaps a Church) and the third to one of the faithful called Gaius. They are short but moving pieces of writing; from Ephesus, where he feels like an exile, the old Apostle speaks to his distant friends in the quiet, affectionate voice of a hoary-headed old man. He begs them in a touching tone of love and

charity to live in union with Christ and in horror of sin. St John
is thus the first theologian of "sanctifying grace", and perhaps
the most moving in his simplicity.

As for the Apocalypse, which St John wrote somewhere
about 92–96, when he was deported to Patmos during the
persecution of the emperor Domitian, this mysterious book
with its jingling words and alternating light and darkness does
more than cry to heaven the protestations and hopes of
threatened Christianity. Its flashing images depict the whole of
human destiny and trace the curve of future history, a destiny
and history whose ultimate goal is the end of time and the
return of Christ in glory, in accordance with the invitation of
the book's last words: "Come, Lord Jesus, come!" It bears
witness to the burning conviction that buoyed up the early
Christians, namely that the Son of Man would soon return, and
also to the eternal Hope that animates the Christian soul in
every age.

THE "PAULINE" GROUP

We now come to another figure, St Paul, who is very different from the beloved disciple, but equally fascinating. Far
from being one of the Twelve like John or Matthew, as a pupil
of the Pharisees he was at first an enemy of the Christians; the
Lord himself had to summon him to his service, in a mysterious
scene smacking of drama and ecstasy, on the road to Damas-
cus, in the hard glare of the midday sun. But as soon as he had
been vanquished by the Light, Saul, now transmuted into Paul,
threw himself headlong into the service of the God who had
laid him low. He made himself into an authentic apostle by
the outstanding quality of his proselytizing, his indefatigable
zeal and his martyrdom.

The New Testament introduces him to us in two ways. On
the one hand, he occupies the foremost place in the Acts of the
Apostles, the last of the Bible's historical books and one of the
most exciting. Written by an extremely well-informed contemporary, none other than St Luke, that cultivated Greek doctor

who was Paul's companion on his travels and also wrote the third Gospel, it is the account, half in chronicle-, half in diary-form, of the great adventure undertaken by the first Christians when, very few in numbers, they set about carrying to the pagan world the message entrusted to them. It is an extremely precious piece of evidence about the period, for Luke was interested in everything, an excellent observer and far from insensitive. But for him, what should we know of the spiritual reasons which determined the loyalty of the first witnesses to Christ crucified? What should we know of that community at Jerusalem which provided the first shelter and storage for the seed of Truth? What could we say about the problems that arose for this primitive Church? How could we write the biography of the Prince of Missionaries, the Apostle of the Gentiles, that St Paul whom so many chapters of the Acts show us at work? No doubt this work by a disciple who had not enjoyed direct contact with the Lord lacks the "gentle and terrible" impact of the Gospels; Christ himself is no longer present, living and speaking divine words; all the same, this picturesque and gripping book is inspired all the way through by admirable faith. Christians have too long neglected it and are returning to it now, at a time when, as in those far-off days it depicts, everything can be summarized in the need for loyalty.

The New Testament also brings us fourteen letters or Epistles by the Paul portrayed at work in the Acts, and they are perhaps the profoundest pieces of writing in the whole Bible. The Apostle wrote them during his extensive travels, when he was in Galatia or Palestine, in Greece or at Rome, at liberty or in prison. He addressed some to Churches or groups of Churches, which explains why they read like encyclicals, and others to private persons who were Christians and friends. From all of them wells up teaching that enlightens the spirit; not academic theology, unfeeling and tedious as it was so often to be, but the science of God transformed into the science of life and death, a theory of knowledge and a supreme revelation. There is scarcely a question that has aroused the interest of the Church in any age that does not find an answer in these fourteen letters, or at any rate the basis for an answer. And what a style! Spontaneous and vivid, it abounds in unforgettable phrases. "Where then, death, is thy victory; where, death, is thy sting? It is sin that gives death its sting..." (1 Cor. 15. 55). Whoever has understood the meaning of these words and many others is far advanced in the supreme study. A giant who changed the face of the world, a genius who drew out of Christ's teaching all that was implicit in it, Paul appears as the man of destiny who enabled Christianity to become the doctrine that was to conquer the world. And from the epistle to the Romans and the two to the Corinthians, Christians of all ages have drawn instruction so rich and ever fresh that twenty centuries have not exhausted its treasures.

THE "CATHOLIC" EPISTLES. THE CHURCH AS GUARDIAN OF THE DEPOSIT

Still other disciples had written letters worthy of attention on account of their spiritual content or the doctrinal authority recognizable in them. Very early, as with Paul's epistles, the custom was established of handing on these precious documents from community to community. The Church has retained some of them in the canon of the New Testament; they are called "catholic Epistles". One of them is by St James—perhaps James the son of Zebedee, the brother of St John, or James the son of Alphaeus, who were both counted in the Twelve; or else James "the brother of the Lord", that is, his cousin, who was the first bishop of Jerusalem[1]—a short, crisp and picturesque piece of writing, reminiscent of the sapiential books of the Old Testament, reminding every believer of the duty of putting his religion into practice, of joining works to faith. Two others bear an illustrious signature, that of St Peter, the Prince of the Apostles; they are powerful, vehement and equally concise and sober. They give the impression of being full of apostolic majesty. One of them is particularly addressed to

[1] Who, according to a very precise tradition, is in any case the same as James the son of Alphaeus, commonly known as St James the Less.

those of the faithful who have had, or will have, to pass through the fire of trial; the other is a moving exhortation to practise the virtues which enable a man to face death without fear, in the certainty of finding mercy. As for the short epistle of St Jude, probably written by Jude "the brother of the Lord", who is mentioned in St Mark's Gospel (Mark 6. 3) but is not necessarily the Jude known as Thaddaeus who was one of the Twelve, it is an indictment, not unlike St Peter's second Epistle, of those Christians who live badly, "changing the grace of God into debauchery", and thus delay the victory of the faith. Behind these writings we can sense the life of the Church, with problems, difficulties and crises not very different from those familiar to us.

With the last lines of the Epistles and the last appealing cries of the Apocalypse the Book comes to an end; the message has been delivered in full and the Revelation is complete. But it is significant and certainly intentional that all the second part of the New Testament should have depicted, either expressly in fact or analogically in symbols, the Society born of Christ properly organized and legitimately entrusted with the protection of the sacred deposit. Guarantor of the truth of the holy text, alone authorized to explain it in accordance with the supernatural illumination bestowed by the Holy Spirit on her first leaders at Pentecost, the Church prolongs the mystery of Scripture in the mystery of her own being. Fundamentally that is what she means by Tradition.

CHAPTER X

THE "MYSTIC MILL" AND THE SENSES OF THE BIBLE

FROM THE OLD TO THE NEW TESTAMENT

The problem that arises for anyone who picks up this compact, complex book with its often surprising vocabulary and mysterious undertones, in whose words the most simple-minded reader senses a supernatural purpose, is that of understanding it. We are all more or less in the position of the high official of the queen of Ethiopia who appears in the eighth chapter of the Acts of the Apostles. When the deacon Philip asked him if he understood what he was reading, he replied modestly, "How could I without someone to guide me?" Tradition answers this expectation and enables the Church to provide replies to the innumerable questions that occur to anyone who takes up the sacred text.

For Christians who read the Bible, the first question is that of the connection between the New Testament, the basis of their faith, and the Old, which at first sight, it must be confessed, looks somewhat disconcerting. What connection is there between the Mosaic precept, "an eye for an eye, a tooth for a tooth", and Jesus' sublime command, "If a man strikes thee on thy right cheek, turn the other cheek also towards him . . . do good to those who hate you, pray for those who persecute and insult you"? It seems as if there is an irreconcilable opposition between the Jewish Bible—especially the ancient parts—and the Bible of Christ.

The problem can only be resolved by reference to the conception, already alluded to several times, of a divine plan, a progressive revelation, a slow but sure ascent of Israel's soul towards the light. It is perfectly true that the two Testaments are conceived on different planes. Jesus himself emphasized this difference when he said at the Last Supper: "This is my blood, of the new testament", implying that the Old was superseded. And St Paul writing to his friends at Corinth (2 Cor. 3. 14) similarly contrasts the Old Testament with the full truth of the New.

However, it would be a mistake to imagine that the two parts of the Bible are simply juxtaposed and quite unrelated; the Church turns its back on this conception by including the books of the Old Testament in the canon of Holy Scripture. On the contrary she asserts that there is a definite and necessary connection between the two parts. In many medieval works of art —in a stained-glass window at Chartres, for example—the four major prophets may be seen carrying the four evangelists on their shoulders. It is a perfect piece of imagery; the New Testament is based on the Old.

First of all, there are resemblances of form. The general style of the Gospels, Epistles and Apocalypse is not so very different from what we are accustomed to in the Jewish Bible. The same intricate arrangement of rhythms, repetitions and alliterations has been traced as in the old texts; it comes from the "oral style". The balanced phrases of the Sermon on the Mount have their parallels in Genesis and the Prophets; the parables so often on Jesus' lips belong to the same family as the *midrashim* of Israel.

Besides, we only have to read the Gospels to see that Scripture plays an important part in the life and thought of Jesus. He was nourished from his youth on this sacred treasury of his people; it was in the Law and the Prophets that he learnt to read. To be sure, he found much more than the spirit of his race in them, he found his Father's work; but it is important to note that he was brought up on these books and continually quotes and refers to them. And that is true of others besides Christ. For example, it has been shown that the sublime phrases of the *Magnificat* which welled up from Mary's pious heart consist from beginning to end of biblical allusions and references.

And what about St Paul? Never did the former pupil of the Pharisaic scholars forget the inspired books of ancient Israel to which he had devoted so many hours of study; his thought and style are soaked in them.

In the actual domain of religious revelation, the New Testament appears as the continuation of the Old. After all, Jesus said that he came "not to abolish the Law", the venerated Torah, "but to fulfil it". His teaching is directly linked to the oldest tradition of his people, for whom the first commandment was "to love God above all else". The second commandment, which the Gospel describes as "equal to the first"—"to love one's neighbour as oneself"—was by no means strange to the Hebrews, for Leviticus (19. 17–18) had already taught it to them; all that Jesus did was to give its real meaning and universal import to a principle that too many Jews restricted to within the narrow limits of their nationalism. The messianic hopes of the chosen people, and their expectation of a Saviour, were taken up by Jesus, who stripped these, too, of their nationalistic and temporal characteristics in order to give them their supernatural significance. If Christians were more familiar with the Old Testament, they would know that the God to be found in it is the same as the one they worship; a God who so loves men that the demands of this love are frightening, who wants us to win salvation "in fear and trembling"—as St Paul (Phil. 2. 12) as well as the book of Tobias (13. 6) says—but is also, in the Old as well as the New Testament, the Good Shepherd (Gen. 48. 15; 49. 24; Isaias 58. 11–14; Micheas 7. 14–15 and many other passages) the attentive and merciful Father.

FROM ANNOUNCEMENT TO REALIZATION

However, even if there is no break or gap between the Old and New Testaments, it is essential to understand clearly how the transition from one to the other takes place. As we said above, Christ himself indicated that an important stage had been reached, the stage of accomplishment and realization. "If the New Testament is contained in the Old," said St Augustine, "it is now the New that gives the Old its full meaning." *Quod*

Moyses velat, Christi doctrina revelat, wrote Suger, Abbot of Saint-Denis, wise minister of Louis VI and Louis VII of France. The formula is to be seen in almost identical form on a statue of St Paul in the church of St Trophimus at Arles: "The Law of Moses hides what Paul's teaching reveals; the grains of corn handed over on Sinai have been turned by the Apostle's efforts into flour." That is the "mystic mill" that Romanesque and Gothic sculptors loved to depict; it can be seen, for example, on the capital of a column at Vézelay.

So between the two parts of the Bible there is more than a difference of climate; that is quite obvious and proceeds from the spirit of love enveloping all Jesus' teaching and radiating from his person, a spirit of love in strong contrast to the Jewish spirit; there is the certainty of an accomplishment, a realization. Israel's revelation, though great, was incomplete and Christ's puts the finishing touch to it; but we cannot understand the Bible if we forget that this ultimate achievement existed in promise and presentiment in the inspired soul of a people that issued from Abraham, and that, in the sacred texts, we can and must discover it.

If it is legitimate and necessary to use the Old Testament to interpret the New, it is much more so to consider the old Covenant in reference to the New; and that is how Christians must read the Bible if they are to grasp all it contains. In this way everything is illuminated and confirmed. The Old and New Testaments, in their double rôle, then form one by the evidence, the progressive completion and the moral support they provide for each other, up to the perfect conclusion and the regeneration of man in God through Christ. That is what made Pascal say: "To understand Scripture, we need a sense which reconciles all the contradictory passages. . . . The real sense is not the Jewish one; but in Jesus Christ all contradictions are reconciled." Similarly Claudel said: "The Old Testament, lyrical or devotional poetry that it is, is incomprehensible without that invisible, approaching presence which arranges and guides it all, down to its shades of emphasis and softest undertones, and creates round it a sort of magnetic field of prophecy. The Old

Testament is incomprehensible without the New." Once again we are reminded of St Paul's words: *Finis enim legis, Christus*.

It is this "magnetic field of prophecy" that we have to discover if we wish to understand the Bible as a unity. The progress of events and instruction right through the book is, as it were, subtended by a supernatural force transcending time and explaining history in advance: the *spirit* of *prophecy*. It envelops the whole of the Old Testament and gives it its true significance. Not only the inspired men known as prophets are endowed with it; all the heroes of sacred history, in so far as God made use of them, enjoyed the privilege: Abraham, conscious of himself as "father of the human multitude", Jacob blessing his posterity before dying, King David, in a splendid psalm, dimly foreseeing his distant descendant, are all authentically endowed with the spirit of prophecy. Everything happens as if, in the divine plan, the Bible were a huge book already in existence before the events it was to describe, to which inspired men had access.

This spirit of prophecy does more than animate the heroes chosen by God—patriarchs, kings and prophets—who have the concrete privilege of foretelling the future. We have already seen, in tracing the curve of Israel's destiny, that before taking shape in the heroes' consciousness, the prophetic intention and significance are revealed in the facts of history; the chosen people is itself, as a whole, a prophetic figure. And again, in so far as the spirit of prophecy colours the whole sacred book, this book itself must be understood as revelation of the future which it contains in germ. In what the Bible reports, in the very terms it uses to report it, we are entitled to try to discern the secret which it has to impart to us.

Especially the one in which all the others are epitomized: that of the Christ, the Messias who brings salvation. The great moral and spiritual ideas which the teaching of Jesus was to formulate definitively had not remained, as we know, in the enlightened consciousness of the chosen people, in the state of pure abstractions; they had literally been clothed in flesh; they had come to life in a being whose shape was projected into the future. This being, the Messias, man's archetype, messenger of the divine will, supernatural agent of Revelation and Salvation, was conceived and carried within herself by Israel and that is her imperishable glory. The duty of Christians, when they read the Bible, is therefore to recognize behind the words and symbols this figure on whom their salvation depends.

The expected Messias—for us, Christ—is foretold all over the Jewish Bible. He is mentioned as early as the third chapter of Genesis—that proto-gospel—and in the blessing of Sem (Gen. 9. 26-7). It is he whom Abraham and Isaac and Jacob glimpsed in the mists of the distant future. It is his glory that is prefigured by the glory of the kings. It is he who is foretold in such precise terms by Samuel's mother (1 Sam. 2. 1-10). Needless to say, it is he who is described by the Prophets properly so called, by Osee, Micheas, Isaias, Jeremias and Ezechiel, and in all his aspects, for in decisive verses Isaias foretells the man of sorrow and his redemptive sacrifice. It is he of whom the Psalms sing, in his victory (2, 78, 110) and in his passion (22, 31, 49). And how many events in the Old Testament only take on their true meaning when viewed in this perspective! The Paschal Lamb that spares the faithful the blows of the angel of death, the brazen serpent the mere sight of which cures the sick, the manna that feeds the wanderers in the desert; all these episodes and many others have a prophetic meaning. In themselves these events may seem to smack of the mere anecdote, even of vaguely animistic or totemistic customs; but interpreted in the sense of the prophecy and the figure, what a mysterious, inexhaustible significance they acquire!

THE THREE SENSES OF THE BIBLE

Understanding the Bible, then, means going further than the literal sense. A sentence of Holy Writ always means more than the actual words of which it is composed; over and above its concrete, literal meaning it awakens echoes, hints at secret truths and reveals figuratively what human language cannot express. That is one of the main premises of the Church's teaching, and the same conviction lies behind various aspects of the liturgy. Jesus himself surely legitimized the procedure when he spoke

of the "miracle of Jonas", who was in the belly of the sea
monster for three days and then escaped, to signify his own
death, his stay in the earth and his resurrection on the third day.
The Church is adopting exactly the same point of view when
she exalts Mary, the Mother of God made man, in the actual
words that the Bible applies to Wisdom, "created from the
beginning of the world and before all the centuries". It is possible to carry this interpretation still further, as the early Fathers
of the Church did with great enthusiasm, and to identify symbolically the destiny of man with the actual events unfolded in
the Old Testament: we are exiled on earth, as Israel was in
Egypt; we are restored to life by going through the waters of
baptism as Moses' people were restored to their destiny by
going through the waters of the Red Sea. The art of medieval
cathedrals is quite incomprehensible except by reference to this
interpretation of the Bible by symbol and significant image.
And it is to this spiritual knowledge of the sacred text that we
are invited to aspire by some of the most imperious phrases in
the encyclical *Divino afflante Spiritu*.

It is customary to say that the Bible has three senses: a *literal*
sense, an *allegorical* or *spiritual* sense and an *accommodated*
sense. People sometimes speak of typical, moral, anagogical,
mystical, figurative and various other senses, but they can all be
reduced to these three. Some writers, by means of a questionable extension of the accommodated sense, limit themselves to
distinguishing between the literal sense and the spiritual sense.
The debate or even dispute between those who emphasize the
literal sense and the champions of the spiritual sense has been
going on for centuries. Just as the literalist school of Antioch
opposed the allegorical conceptions of the Alexandrian school,
so Claudel stood out vehemently against the literalist views of
Fr Lagrange and his pupils at the Ecole Biblique. It is really a
futile dispute; a few moments' thought will convince us that the
spiritual sense cannot conflict with the literal sense which, objectively, contains it; and the most "spiritual" exegesis can have
no other aim, if it is valid and not mere improvisation and

fantasy, than to elicit the inner meaning of a text already sifted by literal exegesis.[1]

An example will make clear what is to be understood by the three senses of the Bible. Let us look at a passage in Numbers (21. 9): "Moses made a brazen serpent and set it up on a post, and if anyone was bitten he looked at the serpent and was saved." In the *literal* sense, that means that the events really happened historically as the words relate. When St John gives us to understand (3. 14–15) that the serpent represented Christ raised up on the cross, we are dealing with a spiritual or allegorical sense. Finally, when Philo of Alexandria writes that the serpent—Eve's serpent—represents pleasure, and that the soul, bitten by it, must turn its eyes to the serpent of Moses to recover health and life, he is using an accommodation.[2]

For the Christian, especially the Catholic reminded of it by papal teaching, his first duty is to know and thoroughly understand the literal sense. In opposition to the over-enthusiastic, even when they were men of genius like Origen, who were ready to throw overboard the literal sense and to retain only the allegory, the Church has given preference to the opinion that Holy Scripture always has a literal sense and that we are never entitled to say that such and such a passage has only a spiritual significance. "Let interpreters bear in mind", says the encyclical *Divino afflante Spiritu*, "that their foremost and greatest endeavour should be to discern and define clearly that sense of the biblical words which is called literal."

But it is also clear that to rest content with this sense is to condemn oneself to stripping the Bible of its richest harmonies, and Claudel is right to castigate the excesses of a too "scientific" exegesis. Away with the "watery breasts of the literal

---

[1] The "spiritual" or "allegorical" sense (the terms are of no importance) is therefore a sense added to the literal sense to foretell or adumbrate a mystery or event in the life of Christ or the Church. Such a sense must be attested by the N.T. or by the virtually unanimous consent of the Fathers and tradition.

[2] For a more detailed discussion of the three senses of Scripture, see *A Catholic Commentary on Holy Scripture* (London, 1953; New York, 1957, Nelson), pp. 53–60. [*Trans.*]

sense"; the spiritual interpretation furnishes richer milk. At this point it must be repeated that to study the Bible as one does the Iliad or the Aeneid, to narrate sacred history in the same way as that of the Hittites or Cretans, is to make a radical mistake, at any rate if one claims to do anything more than provide an introduction to a profound knowledge of the text. We must look beyond the immediate contents of Scripture to the divine plan as a whole and try to understand the economy of revelation. Once again, that is just what we are wisely called upon to do by Pius XII's illuminating encyclical: "Wherefore the exegete, just as he must search out and expound the literal meaning of the words, intended and expressed by the sacred writer, so also must he do likewise for the spiritual sense, *provided it is clearly intended by God. For God alone could have known this spiritual meaning and have revealed it to us.*"

These last words, which we have italicized, seem to be aimed at the excesses of certain *"accommodating"* exegetes, very popular in the East, whose adventurous hypotheses, or rather acrobatics, have long interfered with the really profitable reading of the Bible. To see in the stone which young David projected at Goliath with his sling the "corner-stone" on which Christ's enemies will stumble, or in the staff which he held a prefiguration of the cross carried by Jesus; to see in the scarlet ribbon hung out by Rahab on the walls of Jericho at the time of Josue's attack a symbol of the blood shed by Christ on Calvary: these are bold ideas whose usefulness has not always been very clearly demonstrated. Accommodation may have provided mystical spirits with assistance in their meditations, and some of the greatest saints—St Bernard, for example—have made it yield highly spiritualized results; it is none the less true that it deals in purely human additions to the sense and should be employed with caution. *Divino afflante* recognizes that this approach can render good services in the day-to-day business of preaching, but advises having recourse to it "with moderation and restraint".

CHAPTER XI

THE BOOK OF MAN, TOO

"LOINS AND HEARTS"

Trying to understand both the literal and the spiritual sense of the Bible means, then, seeking to see into God's plan; it also involves coming to know man. Mgr Weber's penetrating description of the Bible as "the book of man and the book of God" cannot be bettered. It should be read and pondered with this double character in mind. A divine book, which did not "fall ready made from Heaven" but was written, in the supernatural light of the Holy Spirit, by men; for that very reason the Bible is a profoundly human book, which awakens all kinds of echoes in the mind of those approaching it with a little intelligence and good will; prisoners in their gaols, invalids in their suffering, travellers and missionaries buried in the depths of hostile countries have times out of number found interest and consolation nowhere but in its pages. It is a never-failing spring at which humanity is constantly slaking its thirst.

The clarity of the Bible is admirable. It sparkles with epigrams, devastating argumentation and analyses unsurpassed in acuteness by any psychologist. He of whom it has been said that "he sounds loins and hearts", when he inspired the authors of the Bible as they wrote the pages, also granted them a share in that total knowledge of the creature, man, which is the privilege of the Creator alone.

It is not only Christ's great definitive precepts that reach straight down to those regions of the mind where there is no further escape from the truth that is justice, where everything to do with man is revealed in all its nakedness: "Let the dead bury their dead!"; "Let him who is without sin cast the first stone!" St Paul's thrilling phrases are almost as striking and penetrating: "a sting of my flesh", "the man of sin" or "this mortal must put on immortality". The books of the Old Testament, too, display this inside knowledge of human nature, which is rich in all kinds of lessons. From it, as much as, or perhaps even more than, from the Greek philosophers with all their mastery of the "Know thyself" technique, flows western psychological literature. It is not for nothing that the wisdom of the nations, nourished on the book of Proverbs, has made real proverbs out of aphorisms like "the fear of God is the beginning of wisdom" or "ill-gotten gains bring no profit". But if we read the whole Bible more closely, we find it full of far-sighted observations. The moving questions of Job face to face with the mysteries of the human condition are our questions, too. "Where does wisdom come from, and where is the place of understanding?" "Why do the wicked live? Why do they grow old, and why are they powerful?" "If a man dies, will he live again?" These questions and many others which perpetually torment us are the ones which the holy man of God puts to himself. And the splendid cries of pain and hope uttered by David, the repentant sinner, are our own cries when the distress of living and despair at being men rise in our throats and choke us. "Lord, I stumble, I am reduced to extreme dejection. . . . I drag myself miserably through the day. . . . However I confess my sin with a sincere heart, for I know that the cause of my anguish is my iniquity. . . . Do not abandon me, O my God, do not remove thy presence from me; help me, Lord, for thou art my salvation!"

A profound knowledge of the human heart, but also the sense of sin, which gives any psychological analysis its real depth, a sense of faith and trial; that is what we find in the Bible, the most human of human books.

THE BEAUTY OF THE BIBLE

The Bible is also human in another way: by its literary qualities and moving beauty. We have already mentioned its variety which, within the framework of a fundamental unity, puts different kinds of writing side by side and thus keeps the reader's interest fresh. The great historical frescoes like Exodus, Kings, Machabees or the Acts of the Apostles, which, broadly speaking, are just as objective as the chroniclers and historians of Greece and Rome, will still grip anyone discovering them for himself and taking the trouble to read them right through, instead of resting content with the fragments that appear in the liturgy or the miserable summaries given by only too many books of "sacred history". The shorter narratives, in which the stories have a moral purpose, *midrashim* like Judith, Jonas, Esther or Tobias, carry the reader along in such lively fashion that modern writers have only needed to transpose and develop them to make them yield subjects for literary works.

As for formal beauty, it strikes the eye on innumerable occasions and in innumerable ways. No purely human poetry has ever been able to rival the sublime inspiration of the Psalms, of whose verses Lamartine said, calling to mind the time when his mother read them aloud on winter evenings: "I realized that that must be how you spoke to God". The delicate freshness of phraseology, so well suited to the violence of the emotions, which forms the charm of the Song of Songs, has never been surpassed by a purely human love song—precisely because it is not simply a human love song. It would be impossible to describe the wonder we feel before the created world better than these words about the return of spring in Palestine do: "Winter is over now; the rain has passed by. At home, the flowers have begun to blossom; pruning-time has come; we can hear the turtle-dove cooing already, there at home. There is green fruit on the fig trees; the vines in flower are all fragrance" (Song of Songs 2. 12). This marvellous, transparent simplicity cannot be surpassed. In a different key, it is also impossible to find greater tragic poetry, expressing man's deepest anguish, than certain passages in Isaias, Ezechiel and Jeremias. And it is doubtful whether the greatest visionaries—men like Dante, Blake, Poe, Hölderlin and Novalis—have ever equalled in intensity of vision the pages of the Apocalypse, but for which, in any case, their work would probably not exist.

For, from this point of view, too, the Bible has endowed humanity with irreplaceable formative material and it cannot be too much deplored that in the educational systems of most of the great civilized countries Scripture does not play as important a part as the literatures of Greece and Rome. In fact, nowadays it is generally granted only a derisory place, confined as it is to brief and quickly forgotten lessons of elementary religious instruction. Classical literature has a valuable contribution to make, but the study of the Bible would add unique and irreplaceable elements to our intellectual training; and since we find in Scripture works containing a synthesis of the Greek spirit and the Hebrew tradition, St Paul's synthesis, the Epistles of the great Apostle of the Gentiles seem particularly suited to act as instruments of that training.

Yet what the literary study of the Bible reveals goes, in a sense, beyond literature. The beauty of a literary work proceeds either from the perfect adaptation of the form to the expression of the thought and feeling—as with western masterpieces—or else from an upsurge of lyric emotion translated into a stream of images that sweeps the form along and expands it, as with the masterpieces of the East. But in the Bible a third factor appears; the beauty does not arise simply from the perfect harmony of form and content or from the subordination of one to the other; all through its pages we detect a reflection, an "aura", an inspiration or, in short, a presence. It is the Word, which was in the beginning as it will be at the end, shining through the text it has dictated, the Word which was made man and took a body, a brain and a voice like ours. Even the beauty of the Bible bears witness to the incarnation.

"FOR OUR INSTRUCTION"

In the Bible, then, man meets himself and marvels; he does more, for from Scripture he receives a constantly renewed lesson. Everything in the Scriptures, says St Paul, was put down "for our instruction" (Rom. 15. 4). Still, it will be just as well to define what we are to understand by that and what kind of instruction is meant.

We must know what it is permissible to ask the Bible and what it is absurd and pointless to ask it. "Does God take care for oxen?" says St Paul (1 Cor. 9. 9), which is to be understood in this way: to know God and love him, it is not necessary to know in which class of animals the bovine family should be placed. Science, in all its forms, operates on a different plane from the Bible; Scripture does not set out to give scientific instruction, but religious instruction. Any intellectual effort aiming at the pursuit of knowledge of creation for its own sake has no connection with what the Bible has to teach us; the real domain of holy writ is not the material world and its method is not that of logic. The two spheres are quite different.

That is why all efforts to "explain" or "justify" the text of the Bible scientifically, or to "harmonize" it with the principles of science—which are transitory, in any case—are merely ridiculous. "The Holy Ghost", says the Encyclical *Divino afflante Spiritu*, "who spoke through the mouths of the sacred writers, did not intend to teach men truths concerning the essential nature of visible things, because such truths were in no way profitable to salvation." Time and time again we have seen the collapse of systems claiming to invalidate or confirm the text by means of astronomy, geology, Durkheim's[1] sociology or, more recently, the study of prehistory. Some of these attempts have left their effects on people's minds; for example, some good Christians still imagine they are defending the truth of the Bible by asserting that the "six days" of the Creation correspond to the periods of Darwinian evolution, to the division of time geologically into the primitive, primary, secondary, tertiary and quaternary ages. Nearer our own time, efforts, just as doomed to failure, have been made to relate the ancient traditions reported by the Bible about the origin of man to the discovery of the fossilized remains of early human races. The

[1] French sociologist (1858–1917) who held the view that "social data exist independently of individual facts". [*Trans.*]

best reply to such attempts is the reminder that it will be difficult to explain how it is that Genesis makes the first smith a
grandson of Cain, whilst the iron age begins about the time of
Josue. . . . As Dom Charlier put it so well: "No conflict and no
accord are possible between the concrete imagery of a faith and
the abstract observations of a technique."

That does not mean that no lessons of a scientific character
can be drawn from the Bible. Scripture asserts that the Creation
did not take place "ex nihilo" or at random; it is at variance
with any philosophy maintaining that reality does not exist,
that the world is a sort of dream, like the shadows on the wall
of the Platonic cave; it implies as a matter of faith the orginal
unity of humanity and is consequently opposed to the hypothesis of "polygenesis", that is the simultaneous appearance of
several human couples at different points on the globe. That is
the subject which at the moment forms the centre of most discussions on the problem of "the Bible and science"; it is by no
means impossible that the solution to this particular problem,
as to many others, will appear of its own accord with the evolution of science and the widening of knowledge.

The radical difference in plane and perspective is no less
striking in the case of the Bible and philosophy. By philosophy
we mean a special discipline, aiming at a different form of
knowledge from scientific knowledge, but equally strange in
itself to the religious impulse, a discipline which moreover is
based on rational principles entirely different from those held
by the inspired writers. So it is absurd to interpret the Bible
according to the intellectual systems constructed by philosophy;
a Hegelian interpretation of Holy Writ is just as pointless—
but not more so—as a Platonic or Bergsonian interpretation.
Of course, in its ultimate purpose, philosophy meets revealed
Scripture again, for all absolute knowledge ends in God; that
is why, from the early Greek Fathers to St Thomas, the thinkers
of the Church worked so hard to put philosophy at the service
of religion. But this harmony between philosophy and religion
arises, not on the level of methods, but on that of faith and

wisdom; and although philosophy claims to pursue wisdom, in the last analysis wisdom proceeds from Revelation.

And that is even true in a sense of theology itself. In so far as theology, too, is a technique it lies outside the province of the Bible; it is quite obvious that the inspired authors of the latter lived in an intellectual climate innocent of the methods and classifications of St Thomas Aquinas. That does not mean that the two are incompatible or contradictory; Scripture offers in the crude state, as it were, what theologians have subsequently classified, thought out and elaborated; but Scripture is much more than any system, for if theology is the "science of God", knowledge of the Bible initiates the reader into a science which is a way of life; it demands more of him than intellectual consent; it demands a commitment, an act of faith.

If Scripture has been given to us "for our instruction", then, it is education of a very particular kind: supernatural, religious and nothing else. And this is just as true of our moral education as of our intellectual or scientific education. Taken as a whole on its face value, the Bible can scarcely be regarded as a handbook of practical ethics; the New Testament contains nothing that conflicts with the principles of ethics, but the same can hardly be said of the Old. If one modelled oneself on some of the kings and important characters in the Bible one would go far; and, even when account has been taken of the punishments that almost always follow the crimes, it would scarcely be advisable to follow certain biblical customs to the letter. In this connection, too, it is essential to look at Scripture as a whole, with the two parts complementing each other, and against the background of a divine plan in course of realization, if we wish to understand the grand sweep of its moral teaching. Many a sentence in Holy Writ, many a lesson to be drawn from the experience and destiny of the chosen people, reminds us that the whole of morality is based on the Bible; there is not a principle, however resolutely secular it would like to be, that did not originate, and often receive its final formulation, too, in Scripture. A society that departs from biblical principles is slipping into the abyss and is near destruction. Social morality, sexual morality, commercial morality, and others, are all there. Ecclesiasticus was long the manual of morality handed to young Christians. "If I had to form a man from childhood as I thought best", said Bossuet, "I should like to make him choose a few good passages of Scripture and to make him read them often until he knew them by heart." And Mgr Dupanloup, who spent a great deal of time on the sacred text, drew this conclusion from his studies: "One closes it armed from top to toe."

The truth is that to anyone reading the Bible, human book that it is, everything that interests man seems to be both definitively formulated and at the same time sublimated, spiritualized and carried up on the wings of inspiration towards a reality transcending the accidents of life and our mortal limitations. The spirit finds in it a climate that encourages expansion and elation. What gives unity, as we have seen, to these heterogeneous books is also what gives its true meaning to the teaching they contain: the presence of the Holy Ghost, the aspiration towards God.

CHAPTER XII

"THIS HUNGER TO HEAR THE WORD OF GOD"

UNDERSTANDING THE BIBLE WITH THE HEART

The fundamental attitude of mind in Scripture—aspiration towards God, love reaching out to him, the ardent desire one day to possess him—is the only thing which can enable us to penetrate its mystery. To understand the Bible, it is not enough to have studied, more or less superficially, a few manuals of sacred history or introductory matter, or to have some knowledge of the higher criticism and Palestinian archaeology. "God did not grant the sacred books to men", says the Encyclical again, "in order to satisfy their curiosity or provide subjects for study and research." There is a spiritual climate which alone makes the reading of the Bible possible, let alone fruitful, if one understands by reading anything more than grasping the superficial meaning of the words. To read it as history or as a treatise is to prevent oneself absorbing the full sense of the history and doctrine it contains. This has been admirably expressed by Maurice Zundel[1]: "You can only understand Scripture on your knees."

So we must approach the Bible and always read it in a spirit of reverence and love. To take reverence first, on opening its pages everyone should repeat to himself the words of the Lord to Moses, "This is holy ground" (Exod. 3. 5), that is, put aside

[1] *Poème de la Sainte Liturgie* (2nd ed., St Maurice, 1934). Eng. trans. *The Splendour of the Liturgy* (London, 1939; and New York, Sheed & Ward).

any empty curiosity and still more—it is hardly necessary to
say this—the cheap humour sometimes derived particularly
from episodes in the Old Testament. But more important still
is love. It is necessary to love the Bible in order to understand
it and to experience before it what was described by Claudel,
who for the last twenty years of his life lived on terms of daily
familiarity with the text, as "a constantly growing sense of
wonder". There is a general law, formulated by a medieval
French mystic, Hugh of St Victor, in these perfect terms: "Love
is superior to knowledge; it is greater than intelligence: we love
more than we understand. Love can approach and enter where
knowledge remains outside." Nowhere can this rule be more
strictly applied than in the case of Holy Scripture. What remains obscure or seems absurd to the scholar is mysteriously
illuminated for a humble Curé d'Ars or a little Carmelite of
Lisieux. "If you want to profit from Scripture", says the *Imitation of Christ*, "read it with humility, simplicity and faith."
More than in any other sphere, the supreme power of comprehension and consent in biblical study is the one Pascal denoted
by his admirable private term, "the heart".

This power of consent and comprehension must be total and
totalitarian; it must control the whole mind. To enter into the
spirit of the Bible it is not sufficient to superimpose on dry
analyses a few pious commentaries; the spiritual attitude of its
heroes and writers, its fundamental intention must be completely adopted. We must listen receptively to the great themes
of the book: the theme of the love of God, the theme of the call
that goes out by preference to those who suffer and are des-
pised by the world, the theme of the invitation to ally oneself
with God and to live at one with him, the theme of God's
infinite mercy and the theme of invincible hope. We must also
experience in ourselves the great spiritual emotions that inspire
the text from one end to the other: the urge to loyalty, anger
against the world's injustices, joy even in suffering and time of
trial. Above all, we must completely adopt that attitude of confident humility and private exaltation defined in the Psalmist's

cry: "Let our raised hands be like the evening sacrifice". The Bible can only be properly understood in the posture of prayer.

PRAYING WITH THE BIBLE

The inspired singer's prayer must be repeated when we read the Bible if it is to awaken all its echoes in our hearts. In the deepest sense of the term, and in many different ways, it is a *book of prayer*. To start with, since Scripture can only be understood by faith and there is no living faith without prayer, the reader is obviously called upon to pray. After all, what is praying but making oneself, in Claudel's words, "accessible to the divine whisper", attentive to the orders and intentions of a transcendent will and mind? And nowhere is it asserted more clearly and more frequently than in the Bible that this will and mind direct the world, and that man's only merit lies in humble submission to them.

The Bible is a book of prayer in other ways, too. If the Church in her capacity of teacher advises the faithful to approach in large numbers and on frequent occasions "this table of celestial doctrine which our Lord has set up for Christian people through the ministry of his prophets, apostles and doctors", it is because she knows that this table is laid with the richest of foods. The comparison with a table—it comes from *Spiritus Paraclitus*, the encyclical of Benedict XV—is already used in a book that cannot be suspected of not aiming at the spiritual nourishment of souls, the *Imitation of Christ*, which speaks of the two tables put within reach of the faithful by the divine Master, namely, the table of the altar and that of Scripture.

Yet it does happen that some devout Christians experience a certain disappointment when they open the Bible. They expect to find uplifting and heart-warming phrases and are faced instead with dry lists of ritual observances, the fierce imprecations of some of the prophets and the enigmatic sentences of the Apocalypse—if not the matrimonial adventures of the kings. It must be admitted that the Bible in no way resembles a manual of devotion; apart from the Gospels and sapiential books, it has little to offer the believer nourished on the *Imitation* or even the *Spiritual Exercises* of St Ignatius of Loyola. The Bible is much more a book of prayer than a book of prayers—a plural which often has an adverse effect on the singular!

However, even from this point of view, it still has a great deal to offer us. First of all, taken as a whole, it forms a method of learning how to pray; it teaches us how to live a religious life. To limit ourselves to the Old Testament only—it is true *a fortiori* of the New—the Bible teaches us that prayer does not simply consist in a ritual (Gen. 4. 7; or Sam. 15. 22; or again Isaias 63. 3–12) but in a state of mind and, still more, in a way of living; that it is not simply a series of well-turned phrases— "let your words be few in number", says Ecclesiastes (5. 1)— but should be, as Jesus proclaims, "Worship in spirit and truth" (John 4. 23). In contradistinction to the superficiality and affectation of only too many devotions, the Bible's prayer is strong, straightforward, sober and virile; the sublimest of prayers, that of Christ, the Lord's Prayer, epitomizes it perfectly.

Strictly speaking, the Bible does contain numerous admirable prayers capable of furnishing the faithful soul with the words of many a devout ejaculation. The Christian's cry of adoration, the *Sanctus*, his cry of repentance, the *Miserere*, his cry of anguish, the *De profundis*, his cry of gratitude, the *Magnificat*, are all taken from the Bible. It is not only on the lips of Jesus, Mary, the Apostles or other leading figures in the Gospel—old Simeon, for example, with his *Nunc dimittis*, or the Centurion of Capharnaum, with his *Domine non sum dignus*—that we find lovely, simple formulas, wonderfully adapted to the aspirations of the soul; the Psalms are full of them, and many are famous. Less familiar are Abraham's prayer of intercession (Gen. 18. 17–33), Moses' supplication after the incident of the golden calf. (Exod. 32. 11–34), David's humble thanks in reply to the promises of the prophet Nathan (2 Kings 7. 18–19), Solomon's glorious and faithful thanks at the dedication of the Temple (3 Kings 8. 22–53), those of Ezechias, Baruch, Esdras and

Daniel, and finally the "Proverb" (30. 7–9) in which the faithful soul simply asks God to let it live in sincerity, simplicity and justice. Prayers of praise and prayers of petition, prayers of repentance and prayers of gratitude, they are all in the Bible; all that is necessary is to go and look for them.

Yet more important than all these separate prayers, beautiful as they are, is the fundamental attitude of prayer revealed and taught by the Bible, the attitude of the man continually striving to realize the highest side of his nature, the man for whom the whole of life is prayer and sanctification. Just as the whole story told by Scripture is subordinate to God and his plan, so all the life-giving nourishment to be obtained from it by man only exists in so far as it is fertilized by God. But that can only be understood by someone who has read and fathomed Scripture as a whole in all its fullness. "Examine the Scriptures", said Christ, and that means not only "understand the meaning of the words", but also "listen to the profound lessons they contain". We must pray with the Bible as a whole.

THE BIBLE, THE CHURCH'S PRAYER

The relationship established between God and the believer by means of the Bible is an extremely personal one: each word has been addressed to me personally; it was I who was summoned to the Covenant with the One God, it was to me that Yahweh spoke on the top of Sinai, it was to me that the prophets promised a "living redeemer" and Christ the resurrection of the body. Nevertheless this relationship also has another character: it is kept alive through the medium of a people, a tradition and a line of descent; it is guaranteed by the authority of a community of which I am a member; it is literally as communal as it could be.

The effort now going on to give back to the Mass its character of communal prayer—a character asserted in so many formulas like the collect and the commemorations of the living and the dead but long neglected—has its logical counterpart in the revival of liturgical prayer, which is essentially biblical.

Liturgical revival and biblical revival go hand in hand. The word of God takes on its full resonance when it is proclaimed during the course of a liturgical ceremony, for it is the communal prayer *par excellence* of the Christian congregation, the prayer of the universal Church looking up to God.

It is obviously not an accident that the choral office consists, by and large, in the weekly recitation of the psalter and that the breviary aims at effecting, during the space of a year, a *lectio continua*, that is to say, a complete reading of the Bible.[1] It is not by accident, either, that the four great Christian festivals—Christmas, Epiphany, Easter and Whitsun—are accompanied in the liturgy by a selection of passages from the most widely separated parts of the Bible, as though to bring home the unity of the divine message. On the other hand, if the liturgy owes much to the Bible, the Bible also owes a great deal to the liturgy: above all, that minimum knowledge of its text possessed by too many Christians who only read it in their missal, but also a sort of permanent topicality, a sort of contact with our hopes and fears, our moods of confidence and anguish. The Church has borrowed many of her prayers from the Bible because she wished to demonstrate the continuity of revelation and her faithfulness to the spirit of God. At the same time she makes her children feel that the spirit that filled the Patriarchs and the Prophets is the same as the one that agitated the air on the day of Pentecost, and that the revelation entrusted to her is simply an endless prolongation of the one received some four thousand years ago in Ur of the Chaldees by a young Semite called Abraham.

Liturgical prayer is the reply to those Christians who are separated from the Catholic community and believe that the Bible, as a direct, personal message from God, makes it permissible to dispense with the Church established by Christ, as if the message had not been delivered to a people collectively organized by the will of God. The early Fathers already knew that much; for them faith in Scripture and faith in the Church were the same thing, not only because the truthfulness of the

[1] Complete symbolically, at any rate.

text was guaranteed by canonical decision, but also because for them tradition was the living Bible, the Bible prolonged by the Church. At a time when this Church, by the voice of her infallible Head, redoubles her injunctions to read and study the Bible, one feels more convinced than ever that it is in the Church and through her that Scripture assumes its fullest import. Her sacraments are to the life of the soul what the sacred text is to the life of the mind: the bread and wine of a more real existence than this one here on earth.

BIBLICAL MAN IS GOD'S FAVOURITE

Such is the Bible, "the book of man and the book of God", the document that preserves the sacred deposit. We said at the beginning of these pages that it formed the foundation of all true humanism and that without it our conception of the world and of man would not be what it is. Now that we have come to the end of this rapid survey of its contents and implications, we can see still more clearly that it is indeed man in all his potentialities who is delineated in it, the real man, he who is not just an animal or a machine, he whose destiny is neither absurd nor hopeless, man fully conscious of his vocation and his significance.

We find in the Bible a conception of man which it is quite easy to define: it is a man who "stands before God" (3 Kings 18. 15; often in St Paul); a man who does not regard himself as the toy of blind fate or obscure and demoniacal forces, but as a factor in the divine plan; a man who knows that he is called by the divine will to a destiny that is unique and not determined by some mathematical law of probability or series; a man who prays, and knows as he prays that he is collaborating in God's work; a man who thinks that the world will improve in proportion to the improvements he makes in himself; a man, in short, who, as he stands before God, is also supported by God, and looks upon this state of dependence as his greatest pride and his greatest hope

Admittedly this biblical man is radically different from the man of Péguy's "modern world", the man who thinks he is free and says so, but finds before him nothing but the void or a countenance with empty eye-sockets speaking the language of the dead. Modern man does not wish to believe, refuses to pray, admits only social and utilitarian laws, thinks the only way of collaborating with nature is by means of vast engineering projects and scientific discoveries and is irritated at the mere idea of being "supported" by an invisible power. But when we see what results this philosophy leads to, what annihilation the process of refusal and negation which we are witnessing is bound to bring with it, the old biblical conception gains by the contrast: it looks exceptionally full of certainty and hope. The Bible is the book of the living God; we know now what it costs to be a man in the age, predicted by a prophet of darkness, when "God is dead".

That is the background against which we must consider the renewed topicality of the Bible; the phenomenon amounts to a protest. It corresponds to an anguish, an expectation. This, too, was predicted in the Bible. "A time is coming, says the Lord God, when there shall be great lack in the land, yet neither dearth nor drought. Hunger? Ay, they shall hunger for some message from the Lord" (Amos 8. 11). And that time of great hunger has come.

TRESSERVE, SUMMER 1955.

Table of Concordant Passages in the Gospels

1. The healing of the paralytic at Capharnaum

Matt. 9. 1–8

So he took ship across the sea, and came to his own city. And now they brought before him a man who was palsied and bedridden; whereupon Jesus, seeing their faith, said to the palsied man, Son, take courage, thy sins are forgiven. And at this, some of the scribes said to themselves, He is talking blasphemously. Jesus read their minds, and said, Why do you cherish wicked thoughts in your hearts? Tell me, which command is more lightly given, to say to a man, Thy sins are forgiven, or to say, Rise up, and walk? And now, to convince you that the Son of Man has authority to forgive sins while he is on earth (here he spoke to the palsied man), Rise up, take thy bed with thee, and go home. And he rose up, and went back to his house, so that the multitudes were filled with awe at seeing it, and praised

Mark 2. 1–12

Then, after some days, he went into Capharnaum again. And as soon as word went round that he was in a house there, such a crowd gathered that there was no room left even in front of the door; and he preached the word to them. And now they came to bring a palsied man to him, four of them carrying him at once; and found they could not bring him close to, because of the multitude. So they stripped the tiles from the roof over the place where Jesus was, and made an opening; then they let down the bed on which the palsied man lay. And Jesus, seeing their faith, said to the palsied man, Son, thy sins are forgiven. But there were some of the scribes sitting there, who reasoned in their minds, Why does he speak so? He is talking blasphemously. Who can forgive sins but God, and God only? Jesus knew at once, in

Luke 5. 17–26

It chanced one day that he was teaching, and that some Pharisees and teachers of the law were sitting by, who had come from every village in Galilee, and Judaea, and Jerusalem; and the power of the Lord was there, to grant healing. Just then, some men brought there on a bed one who was palsied, whom they tried to carry in and set down in Jesus' presence. But, finding no way of carrying him in, because of the multitude, they went up on to the housetop, and let him down between the tiles, bed and all, into the clear space in front of Jesus. And he, seeing their faith, said, Man, thy sins are forgiven thee. Whereupon the Pharisees and scribes fell to reasoning thus, Who can this be, that he talks so blasphemously? Who can forgive sins but God and God only? Jesus knew of these secret thoughts of theirs, and said to

God for giving such powers to men.

St Matthew cuts the story short; St Mark, followed to a large extent by St Luke, is much more vivid and circumstantial.

his spirit, of these secret thoughts of theirs, and said to them, Why do you reason thus in your minds? Which command is more lightly given, to say to the palsied man, Thy sins are forgiven, or to say, Rise up, take thy bed with thee, and walk? And now, to convince you that the Son of Man has authority to forgive sins while he is on earth (here he spoke to the palsied man): I tell thee, rise up, take thy bed with thee, and go home. And he rose up at once, and took his bed, and went out in full sight of them, so that all were astonished and gave praise to God; they said, We never saw the like.

them openly, Why do you reason thus in your hearts? Which command is more lightly given, to say, Thy sins are forgiven thee, or to say, Rise up and walk? And now, to convince you that the Son of Man has power to forgive sins while he is on earth (here he spoke to the palsied man), I tell thee, rise up, take thy bed with thee and go home. And he rose up at once in full sight of them, took up his bedding, and went home, giving praise to God. Astonishment came over them all, and they praised God, full of awe; We have seen strange things, they said, to-day.

2. The healing of the woman with an issue of blood and the raising of Jairus' daughter

Matt. 9. 18–26	Mark 5. 21–43	Luke 8. 40–56
While he thus spoke to them, it chanced that one of the rulers came and knelt before him, and said, Lord, my daughter is this moment dead; come now and lay thy hand on her, and she will live. So Jesus rose up and went after him, and so did his disciples. And now a woman who for twelve years had been troubled with an issue of blood, came up be-	So Jesus went back by boat across the sea, and a great multitude gathered about him; and while he was still by the sea, one of the rulers of the synagogue came up, Jairus by name, and fell down at his feet when he saw him, pleading for his aid. My daughter, he said, is at the point of death; come and lay thy hand on her, that so she may recover, and	When Jesus returned, he found the multitude there to greet him; they had all been awaiting him. And now a man named Jairus, who was a ruler of the synagogue, came and fell at Jesus' feet, imploring him to come to his house, for he had an only daughter about twelve years old, who was dying. It happened that, as he went, the multitude pressed about him closely. And

hind him and touched the hem of his cloak; she said to herself, If I can even touch the hem of his cloak, I shall be healed. Jesus turned and caught sight of her; and he said, Have no fear, my daughter, thy faith has brought thee healing. And the woman recovered her health from that hour. So Jesus came into the ruler's house, where he found mourners playing the flute, and the multitude thronging noisily; and he said, Make room there; the child is not dead, she is asleep; and they laughed aloud at him. But when the multitude had been turned away, he went in and took the girl by the hand, and she rose up. And the story of these doings spread abroad through all the country round.

Three accounts very characteristic of the evangelists' styles: Matthew dry and colourless; Mark extraordinarily concrete, lifelike and moving; Luke more delicate and sober.

live. So he turned aside with him, and a great multitude followed him, and pressed close upon him. And now a woman who for twelve years had had an issue of blood, and had undergone much from many physicians, spending all she had on them, and no better for it, but rather grown worse, came up behind Jesus in the crowd (for she had been told of him), and touched his cloak; If I can even touch his cloak, she said to herself, I shall be healed. And immediately the source of the bleeding dried up, and she felt in her body that she had been cured of her affliction. Jesus thereupon, inwardly aware of the power that had proceeded from him, turned back towards the multitude and asked, Who touched my garments? His disciples said to him, Canst thou see the multitude pressing so close about thee, and ask, Who touched me? But he looked round him to catch sight of the woman who had done this. And now the woman, trembling with fear, since she recognized what had befallen her, came and fell at his feet, and told him the whole truth. Whereupon Jesus said to her,

a woman who for twelve years had had an issue of blood, and had spent all her money on doctors without finding one who could cure her, came up behind and touched the hem of his cloak; and suddenly her issue of blood was stanched. Then Jesus said, Who touched me? All disclaimed it; Master, said Peter and his companions, the multitudes are hemming thee in and crowding upon thee, and canst thou ask, Who touched me? But Jesus said, Somebody touched me; I can tell that power has gone out from me. And the woman, finding that there was no concealment, came forward trembling and fell at his feet, and so told him before all the people of her reason for touching him, and of her sudden cure. And he said to her, My daughter, thy faith has brought thee recovery; go in peace.

While he was yet speaking, a messenger came to the ruler of the synagogue, to say, Thy daughter is dead; do not trouble the Master. Jesus heard it, and said to him openly, Do not be afraid; thou hast only to believe, and she will recover. When he reached the house, he would not let anyone come in with him,

My daughter, thy faith has brought thee recovery; go in peace, and be rid of thy affliction.

While he was yet speaking messengers came from the ruler's house to say, Thy daughter is dead; why does thou trouble the Master any longer? Jesus heard the word said, and told the ruler of the synagogue, No need to fear; thou hast only to believe. And now he would not let anyone follow him, except Peter and James and James' brother John; and so they came to the ruler's house, where he found a great stir, and much weeping and lamentation. The child is not dead, she is asleep. They laughed aloud at him; but he sent them all out, and, taking the child's father and mother and his own companions with him went in to where the child lay. Then he took hold of the child's hand, and said to her, Talitha, cumi, which means, Maiden, I say to thee, rise up. And the girl stood up immediately, and began to walk; she was twelve years old. And they were beside themselves with wonder. Then he laid a strict charge on them to let (continued in column 3)

except Peter and James and John, and the child's father and mother. All were weeping and bewailing her, There is no need to weep, he told them; she is not dead, she is asleep. And they laughed aloud at him, well knowing that she was dead. But he took her by the hand, and called aloud, Rise up, maiden, and she rose up there and then with life restored to her. He ordered that she be given something to eat, and warned her parents, who were beside themselves with wonder, to let no one hear of what had befallen.

nobody hear of this, and ordered that she should be given something to eat.

3. The blind men of Jericho

Matt. 20. 29–34

When they were leaving Jericho, there was a great multitude that followed him. And there, by the road side, sat two blind folk, who heard of Jesus' passing by, and cried aloud, Lord, son of David, have pity on us. The multitude rebuked them, bidding them be silent; but they cried out all the more, Son of David, Lord, have pity on us. Then Jesus stopped, and called them to him; What would you have me do for you? He asked. Lord, they said to him, we would have our eyes opened. And Jesus, moved with compassion, touched their eyes, and immediately they recovered their sight, and followed after him.

Same comments as for the preceding account. It will be noticed, moreover, that the three accounts do not agree in small details: entering or leaving Jericho; one or two blind men (it is true that St Matthew's plural is perhaps purely literary). It is one of those cases in which the traditions followed by the evangelists preserve only the approximate facts.

Mark 10. 46–52

And now they reached Jericho. As he was leaving Jericho, with his disciples and with a great multitude, Bartimaeus, the blind man, Timaeus' son, was sitting there by the way side, begging. And hearing that this was Jesus of Nazareth, he fell to crying out, Jesus, son of David, have pity on me. Many of them rebuked him and told him to be silent, but he cried out all the more, Son of David, have pity on me. Jesus stopped, and bade them summon him; so they summoned the blind man; Take heart, they said, and rise up; he is summoning thee. Whereupon he threw away his cloak and leapt to his feet, and so came to Jesus. Then Jesus answered him, What wouldst thou have me do for thee? And the blind man said to him, Lord, give me back my sight. Jesus said to him, Away home with thee; thy faith has brought thee recovery. And all at once he recovered his sight, and followed Jesus on his way.

Luke 18. 35–42

When he came near Jericho, there was a blind man sitting there by the way side begging. And he, hearing a multitude passing by, asked what it meant; so they told him, that Jesus of Nazareth was going past. Whereupon he cried out, Jesus, son of David, have pity on me. Those who were in front rebuked him, and told him to be silent, but he cried out all the more, Son of David, have pity on me. Then Jesus stopped, and gave orders that the man should be brought to him; and when he came close, he asked him, What wouldst thou have me do for thee? Lord, he said, give me back my sight. Jesus said to him, Receive thy sight; thy faith has brought thee recovery. And at once the man recovered his sight, and followed him, glorifying God; all the people, too, gave praise to God at seeing it.

4. Quadruple synopsis (examples of this are rare except in the story of the Passion)

First multiplication of bread

Matt. 14. 13–21	Mark 6. 30–44	Luke 9. 10–17	John 6. 1–15
Jesus, when he had heard it, took ship from the place where he was, and withdrew into desert country, to be alone; but the multitudes from the towns heard of it, and followed him there by land. So, when he disembarked, he found a great multitude there, and he took pity on them, and healed those who were sick. And now it was evening, and his disciples came to him and said, This is a lonely place, and it is past the accustomed hour; give the multitudes leave to go into the villages and buy themselves food there. But Jesus told them, There is no need for them to go away; it is for you to give them food to eat. They answered, We have nothing with us, except	And now the apostles came together again in the presence of Jesus, and told him of all they had done, and all the teaching they had given. And he said to them, Come away into a quiet place by yourselves, and rest a little. For there were many coming and going, and they scarcely had leisure even to eat. So they took ship, and went to a lonely place by themselves. But many saw them going, or came to know of it; gathering from all the cities, they hurried to the place by land, and were there before them. So, when he disembarked, Jesus saw a great multitude there, and took pity on them, since they were like sheep that had no shepherd, and began to give them long instruction. And	And now the apostles came back and told Jesus of all they had done. And he retired, taking them with him, to a desert place in the Bethsaida country, where they could be alone. But the multitudes heard of it, and followed him; so he gave them welcome, and spoke to them of the kingdom of God, and cured those who were in need of healing. And now the day began to wear on; and the twelve came and said to him, Give the multitudes leave to go to the villages and farms round about, so that they can find lodging and food; we are in desert country here. But he told them, It is for you to give them food to eat. We have no more, they said, than five loaves and two fishes, unless	After this, Jesus retired across the sea of Galilee, or Tiberias, and there was a great multitude following him; they had seen the miracles he performed over the sick. So Jesus went up on to the hill-side, and there sat down with his disciples. It was nearly the time of the Jews' great feast, the paschal feast. And now, lifting up his eyes and seeing that a great multitude had gathered round him, Jesus said to Philip, Whence are we to buy bread for these folk to eat? In saying this, he was putting him to the test; he himself knew well enough what he meant to do. Philip answered him, Two hundred silver pieces would not buy enough bread for them, even to give each a little. One of his disciples (it

five loaves and two fishes. Bring them to me here, he said; then he told the multitudes to sit down on the grass, and when the five loaves and the two fishes were brought to him he looked up to heaven, blessed and broke the loaves, and gave them to his disciples; and the disciples gave them to the multitude. All ate and had enough, and when they picked up what was left of the broken pieces they filled twelve baskets with them; about five thousand men had eaten, not reckoning women and children.

when it was already late, his disciples came to him and said, This is a lonely place, and it is late already; give them leave to go to the farms and villages round about, and buy themselves food there; they have nothing to eat. But he answered them, It is for you to give them food to eat. Why then, they said to him, we must go and spend two hundred silver pieces buying bread to feed them. He asked, How many loaves have you? Go and see. When they had found out, they told him, Five, and two fishes. Then he told them all to sit down in companies on the green grass; and they took their places in rows, by hundreds and fifties. And he took the five loaves and two fishes, and looked up to heaven, and blessed and broke the loaves, and gave these to his disciples to set before them,

thou wouldst have us go ourselves and buy food for all this assembly. About five thousand men were gathered there. So he said to his disciples, Make them sit down by companies of fifty; and they did this, bidding all of them sit down. Then he took the five loaves and the two fishes, and looked up to heaven, and blessed them, and broke, and gave them to his disciples, to set before the multitudes. All ate and had their fill, and when what they left over was picked up, it filled twelve baskets.

was Andrew, Simon Peter's brother) said to him, There is a boy here, who has five barley loaves and two fishes; but what is that among so many? Then Jesus said, Make the men sit down. There was no lack of grass where they were; so the men sat down, about five thousand in number. And Jesus took the loaves, and gave thanks, and distributed them to the company, and a share of the fishes too, as much as they had a mind for. Then, when they had all had enough, he told his disciples, Gather up the broken pieces that are left over, so that nothing may be wasted. And when they gathered them up, they filled twelve baskets with the broken pieces left over by those who had eaten. When they saw the miracle Jesus had done, these men began to say, Beyond doubt, this is the dividing the fishes, too, a-mong them all. All ate and had enough: and when they took up the broken pieces, and what was left of the fishes, they filled twelve baskets with them. The loaves had fed five thousand men.

prophet who is to come into the world.

St John is never content to reproduce the accounts of the synoptics; he adds details omitted by them which are always full of interest.

SELECT BIBLIOGRAPHY

See also other volumes in this part of the series. Works by non-Catholic writers are marked with an asterisk

1. *English Translations of the Bible.*

Rheims-Douay Version. There are many editions of this standard translation.

KNOX, R. A.: *A New Translation From the Latin Vulgate,* Burns Oates, London, Sheed and Ward, New York, 1956.

Westminster Version (ed. C. Lattey, S.J.). A translation from the original tongues which began in 1913. The N.T. was completed in 1935; the O.T. is still appearing. The N.T. and Psalms are embodied in *The Catholic Bible in the St. Peters' Edition,* published by Hawthorn Books, New York, 1958.

New Testament. Translation by James A. Kleist and Joseph L. Lilly. (Bruce, Milwaukee, Wis., 1954).

Confraternity Version. An American translation. The New Testament published in 1941 is an extensive revision of Challoner's edition of the Rheims version. The Old Testament is a translation from the original tongues which began with Genesis in 1948 and is not yet complete (St Anthony Guild Press, Paterson, N. J.).

2. *Introductions to the Bible.*

   A. *General*

   ROBERT, A., and TRICOT, A.: *Guide to the Bible. An Introduction to the Study of Holy Scripture,* trans. from the French, two volumes (Newman, Westminster, Md, 1955).

   STEINMUELLER, J. E.: *A Companion to Scripture Studies,* three volumes (Wagner, New York, 1941, 1942).

   POELMAN, R.: *How to Read the Bible* trans. from the French (Kenedy, New York, 1953).

   B. *Old Testament*

   JONES, A.: *Unless Some Man Show Me* (Burns Oates, London and Sheed and Ward, New York, 1951).

   MCKENZIE, J. L., S.J.: The Two-Edged Sword (Bruce, 1956).

   C. *New Testament*

   LAGRANGE, M. J.: *The Gospel of Jesus Christ* trans. from the French (Newman, Westminster, Md, 1943).

WARD, M.: *They Saw His Glory. An Introduction to the Gospels and Acts* (Sheed and Ward, London and New York, 1956).

3. *Commentaries.*

A Catholic Commentary on Holy Scripture. Contains a commentary on every book of the Bible, thirty-four introductory articles on every aspect of biblical studies and extensive bibliographies. (Nelson, London, and New York, 1953).

KNOX, R. A.: *A New Testamentary Commentary for English Readers,* three volumes (Burns Oates, London and Sheed and Ward, New York, 1953–6).

VAWTER, BRUCE: *A Path Through Genesis* (Sheed and Ward, 1956).

4. *Encyclicals and other official Church documents.*

Providentissimus Deus, 1893.

Spiritus Paraclitus, 1920.

Divino afflante Spiritu, 1943. Published as a pamphlet by the Catholic Truth Society, London, which also publishes a number of other pamphlets on biblical subjects. All the encyclicals on biblical subjects are printed in Vol. I of Steinmuller's *Companion to Scripture Studies.*

Enchiridion Biblicum. Documenta Ecclesiastica Sacram Scripturam spectantia. Auct. Pont. Comm. de re Biblica, Rome, 1954.

5. *Manuscripts of the Bible.*

*KENYON, SIR F.: *The Story of the Bible* (John Murray, London, 1936, Dutton, New York).

*KENYON, SIR F.: *Our Bible and the Ancient Manuscripts* (Eyre and Spottiswoode, London, 1958).

*KENYON, SIR F.: *The Bible and Modern Scholarship* (John Murray, London, 1948).

6. *Historical Background.*

*ALBRIGHT, W. F.: *The Archaeology of Palestine* (Penguin Books, London and Baltimore, 1949).

DANIEL-ROPS: *Israel and the Ancient World,* trans. from the French (Longmans, London and New York, 1949).

DANIEL-ROPS: *Jesus in his Time,* trans. from the French (Burns Oates, London, 1955, Dutton, New York).

7. *Geographical Background.*

GROLLENBERG, L. H.: *Atlas of the Bible,* trans. and ed. by H. H. Rowley and Joyce M. H. Reid (Nelson, London and New York, 1956).

*MORTON, H. V.: *In the Steps of the Master* (Methuen, London, 1934, Dodd, New York).

*MORTON, H. V.: *In the Steps of St Paul* (Methuen, London, 1936, Dodd, New York).

8. *Concordances and Harmonies.*

THOMPSON, N., and STOCK, R.: *Complete Concordance to the Bible in the Douay Version* (Herder, St. Louis, 1942).

LAGRANGE, M. J., adapted by J. M. T. Barton: *A Catholic Harmony of the Gospels* (Burns Oates, London, 1930).

9. *The Synoptic Problem.*

BUTLER, B. C.: *The Originality of St Matthew. A Critique of the Two-Document Hypothesis* (Cambridge Univ. Press, Cambridge and New York, 1951).

10. *Dead Sea Scrolls.* There is already a vast literature on this subject, much of it based on unsound scholarship or coloured by anti-Christian prejudice. The books listed here provide a balanced introduction.

MURPHY, ROLAND E.: *The Dead Sea Scrolls and the Bible* (Newman, Westminster, Md., 1957).

*ROWLEY, H. H.: *The Dead Sea Scrolls and their Significance.* A small booklet giving an account of the finds and a brief review of the various interpretations of their significance up to Nov. 1954.

(Independent Press, London, Allenson, New York, 1955).

*ROWLEY, H. H.: *The Dead Sea Scrolls and the New Testament* (S.P.C.K., London, 1957).

GRAYSTONE, G.: *The Dead Sea Scrolls and the Originality of Christ* (Sheed and Ward, London and New York, 1956).

See also the volume on the subject of the Dead Sea Scrolls appearing in this series.